C

Norway

Front cover: Reine harbour,
Moskenesøya, Lofoten Islands

Right: Heddal Stave Church

TOP 10 ATTRACTIONS

Heddal Stave Church One of the finest of Norway's 29 stave churches *(page 34)*

Pulpit Rock
• Climb to the top for stunning views over the Lysefjord *(page 40)*

The Fjords Some spectacular scenery can be seen around the Hardanger, Geiranger and Sogne fjords *(pages 48, 56 and 59)*

Svalbard The northernmost part of Norway, its islands are a true Arctic wilderness *(page 77)*

North Cape This 307m (1,007ft) cliff is known as the northernmost point in Europe *(page 74)*

Hardangervidda The mountain plateau is now a national park *(page 54)*

Jotunheimen National Park Perfect for summer hiking and winter skiing *(page 57)*

Oslo Norway's capital offers great shopping, fine dining and a wealth of culture *(page 25)*

Lofoten Islands Stay in a fishing cabin on these Arctic islands *(page 68)*

Northern Lights The natural phenomenon of the aurora borealis is not to be missed *(page 86)*

A PERFECT TOUR

Day 1   Bergen

Fly into Bergen and explore the historic Hanseatic Quarter, Bryggen, then take the Fløibanen funicular railway to Mount Fløyen for gorgeous views. In the evening, sail out of Bergen on the Hurtigruten Coastal Voyage for its northbound journey.

Day 3   Trondheim

Arrive in the medieval city of Trondheim and pay a visit to the Nidaros Cathedral, Scandinavia's largest, where Norway's patron saint St Olaf the Holy is buried. For an altogether more worldly pursuit, Trondheim also has excellent shopping.

Day 4   Arctic Circle

Cross the Arctic Circle by ship and arrive at Bodø, surrounded by beautiful mountain scenery. Take a tour to Saltstraumen, the world's strongest maelstrom, before continuing on to the Lofoten Islands in the evening, disembarking at Stamsund for a night in a *rorbu* (fisherman's cabin).

Day 2   Geiranger and Ålesund

Spend the day on board ship admiring the spectacular landscape, including the Geiranger fjord. In the afternoon make a stop and stroll around the Art Deco town of Ålesund, repeatedly voted Norway's prettiest.

N. 71° 10'

IN NORWAY

Day 6 — Troll Fjord

Continue by bus to Svolvær, the hub of Lofoten, and take a boat trip to the magical Troll Fjord, surrounded by sheer cliffs with magnificent waterfalls. In the evening rejoin the Hurtigruten Coastal Voyage, sailing towards Tromsø.

Days 8–9 — North Cape

Passing Hammerfest, the northernmost town in the world, stop at Honningsvåg for a few hours' excursion to otherworldly North Cape, a steep cliff rising 307m (1,007ft) from the ocean. Fly back from Kirkenes, the final stop on the Hurtigruten voyage, the following day.

Day 5 — Scenic Å

Take a bus to the tiny community of Å in the very south of the islands, which is worth a visit for its scenic location and its two interesting museums depicting life on the Lofoten Islands in times gone by.

Day 7 — Tromsø

Visit Tromsø, the capital of the Arctic, home to the Arctic Cathedral, the Polar Museum and the Polaria Centre, before sailing on to the far north of Norway.

CONTENTS

8

31

42

50

63

84

INTRODUCTION

The most accurate observation made about Norway is that it is a land of contrasts: majestic mountains tower above mysterious fjords; harsh winters are relieved by often glorious summers; and long polar nights give way to the radiant midnight sun. Norway offers the visitor a beguiling mix of tradition and modern convenience, spectacular nature and city delights.

Land and People

Situated in the northwest corner of Europe, on the Scandinavian peninsula, Norway is bordered by Sweden to the east, Skagerrak, the North Sea and the Atlantic Ocean to the south and west, the Arctic Ocean, Barents Sea, Finland and Russia to the north. Covering 385,252 sq km (148,747 sq miles) with a latitude ranging from 57° north to 72° north, from south to north, Norway is one of the largest countries in Europe, but has a population of only 4.8 million, or 12 people per sq km (32 per sq mile). The northernmost point of mainland Europe is situated in Norway and one-third of the country lies above the Arctic Circle, including the islands of Jan Mayen, Svalbard and Bear Island *(Bjørnøya)*.

Large parts of Norway are covered by mountain chains, or high plateaux such as Hardangervidda, the largest in Europe at 11,900 sq km (4,600 sq miles). The coastline mostly consists of fjords, islands, islets and skerries, while the east, bordering Sweden, has large forests and lakes. This leaves only three percent as

Bear Island

Bear Island, discovered by Dutch explorers Willem Barents and Jacob van Heemskerk in 1596, is now a protected nature reserve.

The torrent of Kjosfossen waterfall, Hordaland

Tromsø's Polar Museum

arable land, and traditionally many Norwegians had to combine farming with fishing to make ends meet and survive the harsh climate. The sea has shaped the land, not just physically, but in creating the nation of Norway, ancient and modern, from the seafaring Vikings, the long-standing trade in fish and fish products and the more recent discovery of oil in the North Sea at the end of the 1960s. Norway is still one of the world's greatest exporters of fish and seafood, as well as the third-largest supplier of oil.

Some 83 percent of the people living in Norway today are ethnic Norwegians, a North Germanic people. The Sami, one of the world's indigenous peoples, mostly hail from four counties, concentrated in the north, with Kautokeino and Karasjok as the two main centres, both in the northernmost county, Finnmark. In recent years, Norway has also seen an influx of immigrants and foreign workers from a number of countries and some eight percent of the population is either of foreign descent or foreign born.

Norwegian Lifestyle

High taxes have meant excellent benefits provided by the state and a high standard of living. Although the cost of living is comparatively high in Norway, the quality of goods and services is usually first-rate. The majority of modern Norwegians live in or near one of the main cities – Oslo, Bergen, Stavanger/Sandnes or Trondheim – but more often than not they will own or at least rent a *hytte* (cottage or cabin) out in the countryside to which they can escape for weekends and holidays.

You could almost imagine all that sporty energy of the average *nordmenn*, or 'men of the North' as they are known in Norwegian, to be caffeine-induced. Norwegians drink more coffee than most, downing 160 litres (35 gallons) per person per year, and have a fondness for a caramel-like brown goat's cheese, called *brunost*, which provides an additional energy boost in the form of a sugar rush. Despite these oddities, Norwegians are a health-conscious people and research shows that more than 70 percent practise some form of sport or take regular exercise. In summer nothing seems to give a Norwegian more pleasure than to head out into the wilds for the day, hiking boots on, packed lunch made, and quite possibly the youngest family member bundled up and carried on a parent's back – the taste for nature, fresh air and open spaces starts early.

Cross-country skiing is a favourite Norwegian pastime

The northern lights are a spectacular sight

In winter the hiking boots are swapped for cross-country skis, and *långrænn* (cross-country skiing) beats downhill skiing in the popularity stakes here any day. Whether they are city-dwellers or country types, Norwegians take health and fitness seriously at any time of year, taking full advantage of the country's topography and size. There are 2,600km (1,600 miles) of coastline for canoeing, kayaking, sailing or fishing, high mountain peaks for rock-climbing and mountain biking in summer, or Alpine skiing in winter, and endlessly varied scenery of fjords, high plateaux and forests providing awe-inspiring hikes.

Midnight Sun and Northern Lights
The scenery of Norway is one of its main draws for visitors. The stunning contrasts of lofty mountains and glaciers, snow-covered even in the height of summer, the deep gorges of the fjord landscape with crystal-clear bright blue waters, cascading waterfalls and endless open vistas, are enough to take the

breath away of even the most jaded of world travellers. Views such as that from Pulpit Rock, *Preikestolen*, with a sheer drop of over 600m (1,970ft) down to the Lysefjord below, or the Lofoten Wall, as the dark, forbidding cliff wall of the Lofoten Islands is known, are sights that have converted many a visitor into a firm Norway enthusiast. The tiny hamlet of Geiranger, with only 300 inhabitants, receives around 700,000 visitors a year, who come to enjoy the magic and splendour of narrow Geiranger fjord, without the place seeming too crowded. There is always a sense of space and room to roam in Norway.

The climate may be harsh, unpredictable and changeable, but that is part of this nation's charm – fjords and mountains can look even more spectacular when surrounded by dramatic clouds or fleeting swirls of mist. The weather tends to be best from May to August, the most popular time to visit, but the further north you go, the colder it gets. The summer season is short and intense, often with temperatures in the mid-20s°C (70s°F) in the south and up to around 20°C (68°F) in the far north. This is the time to enjoy the midnight sun, a phenomenon best seen north of the Arctic Circle. Depending on latitude the sun does not move below the horizon from May/June until late July/early August. Norway, although still most popular during the summer months, is also becoming more of a year-round destination, not least thanks to another spectacular natural phenomenon, the northern lights, *aurora borealis*, best spotted in October, February and March. The latter are also great months for skiing and other winter sports.

Culture and Tradition

Norway manages to be a very young and a very old nation, all at the same time. Despite centuries of Danish and Swedish rule and

One of Thor Heyerdahl's vessels in Oslo's Kon-Tiki Museum

cultural influence, Norwegians forged a national identity and cultural expressions all their own from early on. For such a sparsely populated nation, Norway has had numerous cultural ambassadors, who have all helped to put it on the world map; writers Henrik Ibsen and Bjørnstjerne Bjørnson, artist Edward Munch and composer Edward Grieg are the best known internationally. During the era of exploratory expeditions Roald Amundsen and Fritjof Nansen further enhanced Norway's reputation, as did Thor Heyerdahl more recently – something to which the Polar Museum in Tromsø and the Kon-Tiki Museum in Oslo are testament. The traditional Halling folk dance from Hallingdal was given a recent claim to fame when used by Eurovision Song Contest winner Alexander Rybak in 2009. Although old traditions are still cherished, Norway is one of the most progressive countries in the world in terms of environmental issues, gender equality and laws allowing same-sex marriage. The country's first female prime minister, Gro Harlem Brundtland, first took office in 1981. Norway is not afraid to go against the current, as has been the case with its whaling policy, which the country still allows on a quota basis; or when voting on two occasions against joining the European Union.

A BRIEF HISTORY

The Viking ancestors of the Norwegians, the Sami peoples, the Danes and the Swedes have all shaped the history of Norway, just as the last Ice Age shaped the landscape, making the country what it is today. For a nation that has spent such a large part of its history influenced by, and in union with, its two Scandinavian neighbours, Norway's identity and culture have nonetheless refused to become submerged, remaining strong until – and since – the country achieved independence in 1905.

Early History

Norway began to emerge from the ice cover of the last Ice Age around 14,000 years ago, and it is estimated that certain parts of the country have been inhabited for at least 11,000 years. The coastline was the first area from which the ice receded enough for human settlement to occur, and by 9300BC people had settled even as far north as Magerøya, near the point of the North Cape, in Finnmark. The oldest Stone Age findings in Norway, from what is known as the Komsa culture, dating from 7000BC, are found in the very north, in Troms and Finnmark, while in southern Norway the Nøstvet, and later the Fosna, cultures settled. These were early hunter-gatherers; agricultural settlements only began to occur around 4000BC.

The Sami, one of northern Europe's indigenous peoples, settled in northern Norway

Viking finds

The Viking Ship Museum in Oslo houses some of the best Viking finds including the Oseberg ship, discovered in a burial mound at a farm called Oseberg, near Tønsberg, west of Oslo. The ship dates from around AD800.

some estimate as long as 4,000 years ago, migrating from
the east to northern Russia, Finland, Sweden and Norway.

The Viking Era

From the end of the 8th century until the middle of the 10th,
Scandinavian people began to play a much greater role in
Europe and even further afield – the Viking era had begun.
While Swedish Vikings mostly headed east in their exploration and raids, Norwegian and Danish Vikings headed
west, setting up trading posts and settlements along the way.
Norwegian Vikings colonised the Shetland and Orkney Islands, large parts of Great Britain and Ireland, the Faroe Islands and Iceland. They even ventured as far as Greenland
and modern-day Newfoundland in Canada. Although the
Vikings initially simply carried out planned attacks on coastal
or riverside communities, they soon began to spend winters
at strategic points, thus making their settlements more permanent, and by the mid-9th century they were controlling
large areas of northern Europe, with a centre at Jorvik, modern-day York in the United Kingdom. This was the beginning

Olaf the Holy

Olaf Haraldsson (995–1030), the man who completed the unification
of Norway, was a descendant of Harald Fairhair, who first began the unification process in the 9th century. Converting to Christianity while in
England, Olaf's mission was not only to Christianise the country, but also
to unify it. Long before this was accomplished he fell in battle at Stiklestad, but soon miracles were reported to occur near his tomb, today
found beneath the Nidaros cathedral in Trondheim, and a cult surrounding him sprang up. Olaf went on to become the patron saint of
Norway. The Pilgrim's Route to Trondheim across Norway reopened in
1997 and was declared a European Cultural Route in 2010.

of the close ties Norway has kept with Britain over many centuries of seafaring and trade. When the Vikings first became a force to be reckoned with, Norway as we know it today was divided into many smaller fiefdoms, where chieftain was often pitted against chieftain and petty, warring factions fought it out among themselves for a power base. The first king traditionally credited with beginning the unification of Norway is Harald Fairhair, or Harald Hårfagre, who is believed to have ruled the coastal and southern areas of Norway from AD872–930.

Olaf the Holy

Unification of Norway

The Vikings travelled to many parts of Europe, coming into contact with different peoples and cultures and also with Christianity. Up until the 10th century, Norway had been pagan; the Vikings worshipping the Norse pantheon of gods. This began to change after Harald Fairhair's son, Håkon, known as Håkon the Good, adopted the Christian faith in Britain. However, Håkon chose not to impose his beliefs on his subjects by force and it was left to one of his successors, Olaf Haraldsson, known as St Olaf the Holy, who became the country's patron saint, to convert the people of Norway, and he was not afraid to use force in the process. It wasn't religion so much as further unifying the nation that drove Olaf, and he is the first king to have ruled most of modern-day Norway, including the north and inland to the east. He

Peter Nicolai Arbo's
Håkon the Good (1860)

died in battle at Stiklestad, near Trondheim, in 1030, and after his death became revered as a saint *(see box on page 16)*. By the end of the century the Christianisation of Norway was complete and no other religion was allowed in the country.

Danish Influence

The 13th century has come to be viewed as a Golden Age. During the rule of Håkon VI, the kingdom was further consolidated and Christianised, with the cities of Oslo, Bergen and Trondheim beginning to flourish. The Orkneys, Shetlands, Faroe Islands, Hebrides and Isle of Man all belonged to Norway at this point in history and there also existed a union with Greenland and Iceland. This was the time when the great kings' sagas in Norway and Iceland were composed, but notwithstanding this, the Viking era of chieftains and fiefdoms was at an end and in the unified kingdom all the sons of a king, including the illegitimate ones, had the same right to inherit their father's throne. This led to a period of civil war in Norway, as well as allegiances and intermarriage to try to secure the throne. When King Håkon VI married Margrethe, the daughter of the Danish king, his son Olaf became king of Denmark in 1376 and upon his father's death also king of Norway, in 1380. This was the start of a long period of unions in Scandinavia. In particular, Norway's union with Denmark was to last almost entirely unbroken until 1814.

The Black Death is believed to have arrived in Norway in 1349 on board a ship from Britain, and its effects were devastating, rapidly killing off some two-thirds of the population between 1349 and 1351. Norway was left weakened and depopulated, and entered a long period of decline. The Queen Mother, Margrethe of Denmark, in 1397 succeeded in uniting Norway, Denmark and Sweden, in the so-called Kalmar Union, a union that lasted almost 140 years, until Sweden seceded in 1536. Norway, on the other hand, stayed in union with Denmark for almost another 300 years.

During this period Norwegian self-rule and decision-making were further weakened, while Danish influence was strengthened. The Danish crown was represented across Norway by governors appointed by the Danish king. The late 16th to early 18th centuries were dominated by wars and the Norway–Denmark union lost territory to Denmark's arch-enemy, Sweden.

Stave Churches

After the Christianisation of Norway in the 11th century, the early missionaries busied themselves with the construction of a number of churches across the formerly heathen lands. These so-called stave churches are medieval wooden structures and the name stems from the building technique of using load-bearing posts in timber framing. In the past there may have been as many as 2,000 stave churches across northern Europe, but only a handful remain today, the majority of which are to be found in Norway. Twenty-nine of these churches are still standing, most dating from the 12th century. Urnes stave church in Sogn og Fjordane is a Unesco World Heritage Site.

As elsewhere, the French and American revolutions inspired hopes for stronger national identity and there was a greater desire for Norwegian independence, but the future had other things in store for Norway before these hopes could be realised.

Union with Sweden 1814–1905

When the union of Denmark and Norway was defeated in the Napoleonic Wars in 1814, Denmark was forced to cede Norway to Sweden, a move that was not at all popular in Norway, where the desire for an independent nation had grown stronger over the preceding four decades. The Norwegians decided to declare independence at Eidsvoll, and adopted their own constitution on 17 May 1814, a date still celebrated as Norway's national, or constitution, day, a major public holiday. The Swedes retaliated and a brief war ensued, but Sweden agreed to accept the democratic Norwegian constitution and a loosely based union with the country, on the condition that the Danish prince Christian Frederik, who had backed the Norwegians, gave up his claim to the Norwegian throne. This achieved, the Norwegian Parliament, *Stortinget*, agreed to elect the Swedish king as ruler of Norway on 4 November of the same year.

Independence

The tide of independence, however, could not be stemmed. In 1905, more than 90 years after first entering into the union with Sweden, it was dissolved without bloodshed. This had been preceded by several years of political unrest between the two countries, and Sweden finally recognised Norway's independence after some 250,000 signatures were collected to support the move. Even before independence, Norwegian cultural and scientific achievements began to blossom as never before, with writers such as Bjørnstjerne

Bjørnson and Henrik Ibsen (who died the year after independence was declared), composer Edward Grieg and explorer Fridtjof Nansen bringing the world's attention to Norway in an unprecedented way.

Foundations of the Modern Society

Norway remained neutral during World War I and it was during the early years of independence that industry started taking off on a more major scale, laying the foundations for the welfare state and modern Norwegian society. The growth of industry and the economy continued during the interim years, but

World War II memorial in Ålesund

during World War II, Norway's neutral stance could not be maintained, with Germany invading and occupying the country from 1940–5. A Norwegian Nazi, Vidkun Quisling, collaborated closely with the German invaders, so much so that the word 'quisling' has come to mean 'traitor' or 'someone collaborating with an occupying force'. Many parts of Norway were severely affected by the war, and the northern towns of Narvik and Bodø, in particular, were heavily bombed. World War II and its aftermath put a seemingly permanent stop to Norway's aspirations to neutrality, and when Nato was formed in 1949 Norway was one of the first nations to join. In 1959 it also joined EFTA, the European

Free Trade Association. Norway's fortunes took another un-expected turn when oil was discovered in the North Sea in the late 1960s. With the oil find, the already high standard of living improved further, and in a referendum in 1972 a small majority voted against joining what is today the EU, a decision that would be repeated more than 20 years later in 1994, when yet again the Norwegians said no to joining.

The 20th century was initially characterised by nation-building, followed by overcoming the hardships of war and finally by taking an active role in European and world politics, on a peace-keeping level. Modern Norwegian politics have been dominated by a long-standing labour tradition, with a mixture of social democratic and liberal values. This has stimulated industry, while also encouraging state intervention and the welfare state, through high taxes. A fiercely independent nation, Norway has maintained its tough alcohol policies and its defiant stance on whaling, a tradition that goes back many centuries, particularly in the north of the country. Norway has one of the highest standards of living in the world, in terms of education, income and life expectancy, and also ranks second in terms of gender equality, according to the World Economic Forum.

A patriotic paraglider takes to the skies

Historical Landmarks

9000BC Earliest signs of settlements recorded in Norway.

4000BC Farming settlements begin to spring up in southern Norway.

Late 8th century–mid-10th century The Viking Era.

AD872–930 King Harald Fairhair begins the unification of Norway.

AD961 Håkon the Good, Harald Fairhair's son and the first king of Norway to adopt Christianity, dies in battle.

1015–28 Olaf II further unifies and Christianises Norway.

1030 Olaf dies in battle at Stiklestad. He later becomes the patron saint of Norway, known as Olaf the Holy.

1070 Building of the Nidaros Cathedral in Trondheim begins.

13th century A brief golden age of stability and prosperity.

1349–51 The Black Death kills two-thirds of Norway's population.

1397–1536 Norway becomes part of the Kalmar Union with Sweden and Denmark.

1536–1814 Norway remains in union with Denmark.

1814–1905 Norway is united with Sweden after Napoleonic Wars.

1905 Norway becomes fully independent from Sweden after the peaceful dissolution of the union.

1914 The country remains neutral during World War I.

1918 Norwegian women gain the right to vote.

1940–5 Germany occupies Norway during World War II.

1949 Norway joins Nato.

1968–9 Oil exploration and the discovery of oil in the North Sea. Production begins in 1971.

1972 Norway votes against joining the EU.

1981 Gro Harlem Brundtland becomes Norway's first female prime minister, leading a Labour government.

1994 Norway votes for the second time against joining the EU. Hosts the Winter Olympic Games in Lillehammer.

2008 Norway's first opera house opens in Oslo.

2010 The Norwegian Nobel committee anger China by awarding the Peace Prize to Chinese political prisoner Liu Xiaobo.

BRESTUA

PRINS OLAVSV

SVARTISEN

WHERE TO GO

In Norway you find yourself running out of superlatives: there just aren't enough of them to cover the natural wonders of the scenery. From the understated charm of the white-painted villages of the southern coastline, to the stark, barren beauty of the Arctic north, Norway has a lot to offer intrepid travellers, particularly those with a penchant for the great outdoors. The cities of Oslo, Bergen, Stavanger and Trondheim are big enough to be interesting and varied, but small enough to get around and feel at home in, and even here nature is never far away. The landscape is ever-changing in a country that runs for 1,752km (1,089 miles) from north to south, encompassing mountains, forests, glaciers, lakes, tundra and, most famous of all, the Norwegian fjords.

OSLO

The Norwegian capital, founded in 1048, lies on the waters of the Oslo Fjord with a bustling harbour. Mountains serve as a backdrop and the Great Outdoors never seems far away even in the centre, with its leafy parks. The main artery, Karl Johans Gate, partly pedestrianised, runs through the centre, connecting many of the major sights and places of interest.

Central Oslo

With 590,000 inhabitants, **Oslo** is by far the most populous city in Norway, but the centre is compact and easy to get around. The best way to see the sights is on foot, and the **Central Station** (Sentralstasjon) makes a good starting point since this is also where you find the main tourist office (*see*

Svartisen Glacier

page 131). Outside the station is the start of **Karl Johans Gate**, affectionately known just as 'Karl Johan', the 1km (½-mile)-long main street that runs through the centre up to the Royal Palace, passing many of Oslo's main sights. The first half is a pedestrianised zone, running uphill to the

B ▶ **Cathedral** (Domkirke; Stortorvet 1B; daily 10am–4pm; free) only two blocks from the station. The cathedral may appear unassuming from the outside, but it's worth a peek inside for the colourfully painted ceiling and stained-glass windows, designed by Emmanuel Vigeland. Surrounding the cathedral is an old bazaar dating from the middle of the 19th century. Today it's full of quirky shops, selling trendy clothes and jewellery, and there are cafés and restaurants with outdoor seating in summer. The pedestrianised part of Karl Johan is lined with shops ranging from the tackiest of souvenir stands to designer labels – as a rule, the further away from the railway station, the more up-market.

C ▶ Starting at the **Norwegian Parliament** (Stortinget; www.stortinget.no; guided tours in English and Norwegian, Sat 10am, 11.30am and 1pm; charge), Karl Johan becomes a wide boulevard. The parliament building has been the seat of the National Assembly since 1866, when Norway was still in union with Sweden, and it is partly open to the public. Eidsvolls Plass, parallel to Karl Johan, has lovely fountains playing in summer and an ice rink in winter. It leads down to the **National Theatre** (Nationaltheatret), with **Oslo University** (Universitet) opposite. Straight ahead at the end of Karl Johan, facing the parliament, lies the serene **Royal Palace** (Kongelige ◀ **D** Slottet; www.kongehuset.no; guided tours in English in

Christmas market

In the weeks leading up to Christmas, Rådhusplassen, in front of the City Hall and the Nobel Peace Center, plays host to a large Christmas market, selling handicrafts from all over Norway.

The imposing Norwegian Parliament building

summer, times vary; charge) a large building in muted yellows with clean Nordic lines, surrounded by the abundant parklands of the Slottsparken.

Across Slottsparken, another of Oslo's main thoroughfares, Henrik Ibsens Gate, leads to **Munkedamsveien**, a street with stroller-friendly pavements, nice shops, cafés and bars, running down to **Filipstad Brygge** and **Tjuvholmen**, both part of an ambitious waterfront development project. Next door is **Aker Brygge**, a former shipyard that has been completely regenerated, turning it into one of Oslo's best places to shop, eat and drink. It houses more than 70 shops and 40 eateries from fast food to fine dining and, situated right on the harbour, is positively buzzing on summer nights. A walk along the harbour promenade offers good views over the harbour and fjord where you can pick up sightseeing boats and cruises. Not far away, on Rådhusplassen, lies the **Nobel Peace Center** (Nobels Fredssenter; June–Aug daily

10am–6pm, Sept–May Tue–Sun; charge), telling the history of the prize and offering exhibits on war, peace and conflict resolution. Close by is the **City Hall** (Rådhuset). A short walk east is **Akershus Fortress and Castle** (Slott og Festning; daily 6am–9pm, changing of the guard 1.30pm; free), a 13th-century fortress built to protect Oslo from attack. Close by, the Resistance Museum (Hjemmefrontmuseum) illustrates the intense story of occupied Norway, while the Armed Forces Museum (Forsvarsmuseet) to the south covers military and political history from the Vikings to the present. Also in the vicinity are the **Museum of Contemporary Art** (Museet for Samtidskunst) and the **Fearnley Museum of Modern Art**, both with excellent collections.

Still in the south is the magnificent waterside **Opera House**, which opened in 2008 and has won an array of prestigious architectural awards. Continuing north, **Christiania Square**, one of the oldest squares in Oslo, is surrounded by quaint buildings, some dating from the 17th century. Akersgata street leads back to Karl Johans Gate, north of which, on Universitetsgaten, is the **National Gallery** (Nasjonalgalleriet; Tue–Fri 10am–6pm, Sat–Sun 11am–5pm; charge), with a great collection of works by Norwegian artists.

Café culture in Aker Brygge

East and South Oslo
Former working-class and immigrant areas in east Oslo, such as Rodeløkka, Grünerløkka and Grønland, have become hip and happening. The most interesting is Grünerløkka, easily reached from the National Theatre by tram *(trikken)* No. 13, which

runs right through the district. This is a place to amble, soak up the atmosphere and check out the quirky boutiques, international grocery stores, organic food shops, unusual eateries and quiet residential areas. Thorvald Meyers Gate is the main street and Birkelunden park with the Paulus Church is pleasant.

Southeast of Grünerløkka, through Sofienberg Park, past the Sofienberg Church, lies the area of **Tøyen**, home to some excellent museums, clustered together and surrounded by the lush **Tovenhagen Botanical Gardens**.

The 13th-century Akershus Fortress and Castle

The Palaeontological, Zoological, Geological and Natural History Museums can all be found here (times vary; charge). The gardens themselves are worth a visit, especially for the aromatic herb garden. Opposite the garden entrance lies another of the city's best museums, the **Munch Museum** (Munch-museet; www.munch.museum.no; June–Aug daily 10am–6pm, Sept–May Tue–Fri 10am–4pm, Sat–Sun 11am–5pm; charge), with a collection of Munch's paintings.

West and North of the City

The Majorstua area (tram No. 19 from the National Theatre) also has interesting shops and cafés. From Majorstua tram and underground station it's a short walk to the **Vige-**

land Sculpture Park (Vigelandsparken), with more than 200 statues made by Gustav Vigeland (daily 24 hours; free). His studio is now the Vigeland Museum (Tue–Sun 11am–5pm; free). The City Museum and a museum dedicated to ice-skating are here, too. A 30-minute stroll down Frognerveien, with grand old houses, cafés and restaurants, takes you back to the centre of town.

Oslo's other museum area is the **Bygdøy Peninsula**, which can be reached by boat (No. 91; services May–Oct) from the City Hall pier. Bygdøy is home to the **Norwegian Folk Museum** (Norsk Folkemuseum), an

Playing in the snow at the Holmenkollen ski jump

indoor/outdoor venue devoted largely to rural culture; the **Fram Museum** (Frammuseet) housing Fridtjof Nansen's polar sailing ship *Fram*; and the **Kon-Tiki Museum** (Kon-Tiki Museet), opposite which is the **Maritime Museum** (Norsk Sjøfartsmuseum; all museum times vary). To the south, on Huk Aveny, is the **Holocaust Center**, in the mansion occupied by traitor Vidkun Quisling in World War II.

To the north, **Holmenkollen** (www.holmenkollen.com), with the ski jump, arena and world's oldest ski museum, is one of Oslo best-loved attractions, and nearby **Frognerseteren** has some of the best views of Oslo and the fjord from the mountain lodge (www.visitoslo.com).

THE SOUTH AND SOUTHEASTERN BORDERLANDS

Southern Norway is characterised by a rocky coastline teeming with islands, islets and skerries, many of which are popular summer holiday spots for Norwegians. The coast is dotted with pretty towns and villages with white-painted houses. Further inland lie some of Norway's richest farmlands, while to the east forests spread across the border with Sweden.

Southern Coast

Travelling out of Oslo, along the Oslo fjord, is **Tønsberg**, some 100km (62 miles) south. On the surface Tønsberg does not appear to have much of interest, but this town, the oldest in Norway, has a rich history going back over 1,100 years and is worth a stop for its 13th-century castle ruins and Viking-era grave mounds. It is also famed as the home of *Jarlsberg* cheese. **Oslo Torp** airport is nearby and there are direct connections by ferry from Sandefjord to Strömstad in Sweden.

Passing Sandefjord and Larvik on the E18, the main Oslo–Stavanger highway, **Kragerø** is the first picturesque whitewashed village of note, followed by **Risør**, known as the 'White town on the Skagerrak'. The former was the favourite haunt of artists such as Edvard Munch, while the latter has beautifully preserved 17th-century houses. Both have a variety of accommodation and restaurants.

Cycling in Kristiansand

Continuing south, **Arendal** is one of the larger towns along the coast, worth a visit for its old district, **Tyholmen**.

Grimstad, another white-painted coastal town further south, is said to have the most hours of sunshine in Norway. In the 19th century, Grimstad was one of the greatest shipbuilding centres in the world, and the Maritime Museum (May–Sept Mon–Sat 11am–5pm, Sun 1–5pm; charge) provides fascinating insights into this aspect of the town. West of Kristiansand *(see below)* lies Norway's southernmost town **Mandal**, followed by the country's southernmost point, **Lindesnes**, with a lighthouse and museum (tel: 38-25 54 20; May–Sept daily, Oct–Apr Sat–Sun only, times vary).

Kristiansand

3 ▶ **Kristiansand** is the largest city in southern Norway and the fifth largest in the country. Situated at the southern end of Norway, 330km (205 miles) from Oslo, it is the hub of the south with ferry connections to Denmark. The town centre is known as **Kvadraturen** and encompasses most of the sights of note, including the **Fish Market** (Fiskebrygga; Mon–Sat 8am–5pm) near the small harbour along the quayside. The market is a good place to soak up the atmosphere and grab a nice, fishy lunch at one of the eateries.

One of the most prominent features of Kristiansand is the **Christiansholm Fortress**, an imposing structure from 1672, set right on the seafront promenade, amid extensive lawns, attracting sun worshippers in summer. Heading east from the fortress, the city has its own beach, **Bystrand**, also popular when the weather allows. Away from the seafront, five blocks along Kirkegata, lies the city's **Cathedral**, the third largest in Norway, with capacity for 1,800 people. A short walk northeast is the old part of town, **Posebyen**, with buildings dating from the 17th–19th centuries. The 14 blocks of low-rise wooden houses are perfect for a quiet stroll.

One of the main attractions of the region lies 9km (5½ miles) east of the centre. **Kristiansand Zoo and Amusement Park** *(see Activities for Children, page 94)* is a major draw for the whole family.

Exploring Inland

Inland from the coast, 80km (50 miles) west of Oslo, **Kongsberg**, founded in 1624, is known for its old silver mine. The last mine was closed in 1957, but there is plenty of silver history to experience and explore here. At Hyttegata 3, the fascinating **Mining Museum** (Norsk Bergverksmuseum; tel: 91-91 32 00; www.norsk-bergverksmuseum.no; mid-May–Aug daily 10am–5pm, Sept–May times vary; charge) has a wealth of information on the era, and it is also possible to visit the **Royal Silver Mines** on guided tours, about which the museum has more information.

Heddal Stave Church

Continuing west along the E134 you will reach the largest preserved stave church in Norway, **Heddal Stave Church** (www.heddalstavkirke.no; daily June–Aug 9am–7pm, May and Sept 10am–5pm, but closed Sun am if there is a service; charge). There is a café and an outdoor museum.

To the south, in Telemark, the **Telemark Canal**, a 105km (65-mile) stretch of lakes and a man-made canal, connecting Skien and Dalen through 18 locks, is a picturesque boat journey, taking a leisurely 11 hours (www.visittelemark.com).

North of Dalen, along highway 37, **Rjukan**, in the shadow of Telemark's highest peak, Gausta, has become something of an outdoor activities and adventure sports centre. This is the place to try Alpine and cross-country skiing, ice climbing and ski-sailing in winter, bungee-jumping, rock climbing, archery and horse riding in summer, among many other things (www.visitrjukan.com).

Rjukan is a great place to try cross-country skiing

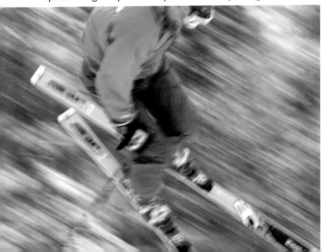

Southeastern Borderlands

The region of Østfold, between the Oslo fjord and the Swedish border, is an area steeped in history, as evidenced by its strong fortifications, hailing from a time when relations between Norway, Sweden and Denmark were less neighbourly and far more belligerent.

Fredrikstad, 90km (56 miles) southeast of Oslo, on the Oslo fjord and River Glomma, is perhaps the best preserved fortress town in Scandinavia. The **Kongsten Fortress** dates back to 1685, when Norway was in union with Denmark, whose arch-enemy Sweden was only a stone's throw away. **Gamlebyen** is the name of the old town, also dating from the 17th century, with a number of historic buildings, a drawbridge, moat and fortifications. Nearby **Halden**, almost waving distance from Sweden, less than 10km (6 miles) away, is another town with a formidable fort. **Fredriksten Fortress** (tel: 69-18 54 11; mid-May–Aug 10am–5pm, grounds 24 hours year-round; guided tours available; charge) sits on a hilltop overlooking Halden itself. Built in 1661, in its heyday it withstood six Swedish sieges without ever being captured. At the southeasternmost point of Norway a new marine national park, **Ytre Hvaler** (www.ytre-hvaler.no), opened in 2009.

STAVANGER AND AROUND

Stavanger, in the county of Rogaland, is Norway's third-largest city, including nearby Sandnes and the metropolitan area. It was near here that the unification of Norway began with Harald Fairhair, and in more modern times Stavanger was often the last that the 900,000-odd Norwegians who emigrated to North America saw of their nation. The sea has played a prominent part in Stavanger's history – there are strong links with Britain across the North Sea and the city is also the headquarters of the Norwegian oil industry. The fjord scenery in the surroundings is some of the country's most spectacular, and Pulpit Rock on the Lysefjord is something that every visitor must see.

Central Stavanger

Most of the sights in Stavanger are concentrated within easy walking distance of each other. In the very centre of town, near the railway station, lies **Breiavatnet**, a lovely lake with fountains, surrounded by pleasant buildings, some of which serve coffee and cakes. Just to the north of Breiavatnet is the city park and **Stavanger Cathedral** (Domkirken; June–Aug daily 11am–7pm, Sept–May Tue–Thur and Sat 11am–4pm; free), built in 1125 in Anglo-Norman style. The tourist information office can be found just behind the cathedral (Domkirkeplassen 3; tel: 51-85 92 00). From here, a short

Going West

Organised emigration from Norway to North America began in 1825, when the ship *Restauration* set off from Stavanger for New York City. Upon arrival it was impounded for exceeding the declared passenger limit – one passenger had given birth during the 98-day voyage – and the captain had to spend two weeks in jail for the offence. Between 1825 and 1925 well over 800,000 Norwegians, roughly one-third of the population, left for North America, and today there are some 5 million Norwegian-Americans, ie more than there are Norwegians in Norway itself. The majority settled in the Midwest, with Minnesota, Wisconsin and the Dakotas having the highest percentage of Norwegian descendants. In North Dakota, for example, more than 30 percent of the population have Norwegian roots. Some 40,000 people still speak Norwegian in the home across North America, and Norwegian culinary traditions and cultural expressions live on, on the other side of the Atlantic.

Detail of Stavanger Cathedral

walk leads down to the harbour on the inlet of **Vågen**. Stavanger's waterfront is a bustling place, lined with restaurants, bars and cafés, as well as the boats moored in the guest harbour. It is a nice place to eat alfresco in summer, and also the site of Stavanger's annual summer food festival, *Gladmat (see box on page 97)*. Northeast, behind the harbour, lies an area of cobbled streets, unusual shops and boutiques, with an ever-so-slightly bohemian feel to it.

This area is also home to **Valbergtårnet** (mid-June–mid-Aug daily 11am–3pm), a mid-19th-century watchtower built to protect Stavanger from fires. Sadly the original watchtower, which was made of wood, burnt to the ground and was replaced by the current one, built of stone. A few blocks east of Valberget, the quayside is home to the **Petroleum Museum** (Norsk Oljemuseum; www.norskolje.museum.no; June–Aug daily 10am–7pm, Sept–May Mon–Fri 10am–4pm, Sun 10am–6pm; charge), dedicated to all things oily.

Summer festivals

Summer is festival time in Stavanger with more than 100 events, including full-moon concerts, an international tattoo convention, shooting championships, and much more (www.regionstavanger.com).

You can even experience life on an oil rig here and find out about Norway's recent history as an oil producing nation (see box page 41). Geoparken, next to the museum, has everything for the modern child, from skateboarding facilities to sand volleyball.

Old Stavanger

On the western side of the Vågen inlet lies what remains of the **Old Town**, 173 well-preserved wooden buildings mostly from the turn of the 18th century. Where the old town begins, along the quayside lies the **Maritime Museum** (Sjøfartsmuseet; www.stavanger.museum.no; June–Aug daily 11am–4pm, Sept–May Sun 11am–4pm; charge), and further along the same quay, the **Norwegian Emigration Centre** (Det Norske Utrandrersenteret; Mon–Fri 9am–3pm), charting the history of Norwegian emigration (see box page 36).

Another unusual museum in the old town is the one dedicated to the canning industry. The **Canning Museum** (Norsk Hermetikkmuseum; Øvre Strandgt. 88 and 90; www.stavanger.museum.no; June–Aug daily 11am–4pm, Sept–May hours vary; charge) is located in an old canning factory and there are former workers' cottages also open to the public in summer. In its heyday in 1925, Stavanger had 58 such factories, the majority of them canning sardines. The old town in general is lovely for a stroll around the pretty wooden houses with their well-tended gardens. Bear in mind, though, that this is not a living museum: many houses are inhabited by Stavanger citizens, who don't always appreciate visitors peeking too closely through their windows.

Art and Culture

In many parts of Stavanger a number of seemingly random cast-iron figures can be spotted. The **Broken Column** by English artist Antony Gormley is a huge project consisting of 23 cast-iron sculpted figures, all 1.95m (6ft 4in) tall and cast, like all his figures, from his own body. The first one is at Rogaland Art Museum, 41m (135ft) above sea level, the final one stands on rocks *below* sea level. They can be found in the cathedral churchyard, in a swimming pool, a car park, a school yard, and there is even one in a private home.

Another cultural project, which has been running since 2008 when Stavanger was designated European Capital of Culture, is **Norwegian Wood**, focusing on Stavanger as Europe's largest timbered city – it has more than 8,000 wooden houses. It includes 15 building projects, designed with an environmentally friendly ethos.

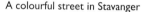

A colourful street in Stavanger

It's a steep hike to the top of Pulpit Rock

Around Stavanger

The town of **Sandnes**, 12km (7½ miles) to the south, is considered part of the Stavanger/Sandnes metropolitan area. From here it is a short drive to one of Norway's most spectacular fjords and perhaps the best-known view in the country – the **Lysefjord** seen from **Pulpit Rock** (Preikestolen). ⑤ The Lysefjord and Pulpit Rock mountain lodge, which opened in 2008, can both be reached by car or boat from Sandnes, or by ferry and bus or car from Stavanger via Tau, from May to September. From base camp at the mountain lodge a marked trail leads up to the rock itself, a two- to three-hour climb that can be very steep in places and should only be attempted if you are reasonably fit and wearing strong shoes. Those who do make the hike are rewarded by stunning panoramic views, but the 604m (1,982ft) -high cliff is not for the faint-hearted. Lying face-down at the edge of the cliff, spotting the sightseeing boats far below, is very popular if slightly vertigo-inducing. Those of a less adventurous or energetic bent can choose to view the rock and the fjord from a fjord cruise, which can be taken year-round, whereas the hiking trail is only safe for five months of the year (Rødne Fjord Cruise does three-hour cruises on the Lysefjord; www.rodne.no).

Medieval Bryggen is a World Heritage Site

gorgeous views across Bergen (www.floibanen.no; Mon–Sat
8am–11pm, Sun 9am–11pm, summer until midnight;
charge). The journey to the top takes only 5–7 minutes, and
there is a café open daily in summer, at weekends during the
rest of the year. Fløibanen is best enjoyed in good weather,
and since Bergen's climate is extremely unpredictable, if the
sun's out, it's best to take advantage.

Central Bergen and Nordnes Peninsula

Between the Fish Market and the Fløibanen Funicular lies
the **Church of the Holy Cross** (Korskirken), originally medieval but now largely Renaissance; and a short walk east,
the **Cathedral** (Domkirke), which, despite its medieval origins, has been rebuilt five times because of fires. In the same
street, Kong Oscars gate, lies the unusual Leprosy Museum
(Lepramuseet). Bergen once had a huge concentration of leprosy patients, and the bacillus was discovered here in 1873

by Armauer Hansen. Running parallel is Kaigaten, bordered by Lille Lungegårdsvann, the attractive city park, with a small lake and a pavilion. The grand **Grieghallen** concert hall lies on the other side of the park. Externally, it resembles a grand piano; internally, the acoustics are marvellous.

Southwest of Lille Lungegårdsvann, in the university distict, are a number of interesting museums: the Natural History Museum (Naturhistorisk) set in a botanic garden; the Cultural History Museum (Historisk) with information on stave churches; and the Maritime Museum (Sjøfartsmuseet). Heading northwest, onto **Nordnes Peninsula**, along Strandgaten, is New Church (Nykirken), the first church in Bergen to be built as Lutheran, rather than converted from Catholicism. At the tip of the peninsula lies the **Aquarium** (Akvariet; www.akvariet.no; times vary; charge), with a new tunnel where you can get extra close to the sharks.

Edvard Grieg

Norway's most famous composer, Edvard Grieg (1843–1907), was partly of Scottish descent. His father's grandfather hailed from Aberdeenshire in Scotland in the 18th century and four generations of Griegs (then spelled 'Greig'), including Edvard's father, held the post of British consul in Bergen. Edvard, on the other hand, decided on a different career path. Growing up in a musical home, he enrolled at the conservatory in Leipzig, Germany, where he finished his studies in 1862. He is perhaps best known for having composed the music for his friend Henrik Ibsen's play *Peer Gynt* in 1874–6. Among his other illustrious friends were Franz Liszt and Pyotr Tchaikovsky. Grieg set to music the lyrics of several poems by Goethe, Ibsen, Kipling and others, and wrote a number of songs. He married his first cousin Nina in 1867 and their home, Troldhaugen outside Bergen, is now open to the public (see page 47). He died aged 64 after a long period of illness.

Around Bergen

Troldhaugen (www.troldhaugen.com; daily May–Sept 9am–6pm, Oct–Apr 10am–4pm; guided tours available; charge) was the home of composer Edward Grieg and his wife Nina. It is situated a 20-minute bus ride south of Bergen, on a peninsula overlooking Nordsåsvatnet inlet. The house is just as he left it, with his piano in working order. There is also a small museum and a concert hall that can be visited; during summer there are concerts and recitals (Wed, Sat and Sun). The grave of Edward and Nina Grieg is embedded in the rock face near the house. On a clear day the views from Troldhaugen are lovely.

Several of the mountains surrounding Bergen can be reached by funicular or cable car. The summit of 643m (2,109ft) Ulriken mountain can be reached by a cable-car trip, the **Ulriken643 Panorama Tour** (daily May–Sept 9am–9pm, Oct–Apr until 5pm; charge). Buses take visitors from the Fish Market to the cable car for stunning views across the city, islands and fjordlands beyond. There are 15 different hiking trails and circular routes when you get to the top, and other activities to choose from include climbing, abseiling and paragliding, as well as winter sports; and there is also a good restaurant.

The Fløibanen Funicular Railway on its way up to Fløyen

Hardangerfjord

Fantoft Stave Church (Fantoftveien, Paradis, 6km/4 miles south of the city centre; bus stop and car park at Birkelundsbakken; mid-May–mid-Sept daily 10.30am–6pm; charge) is one of the few stave churches to be found within the limits of a large city. The original was constructed in the village of Fortun in Sogn county in 1150 and moved to its current location in 1883. It was burnt down in 1992 in an arson attack, but has been beautifully rebuilt as it was before the fire.

Hardangerfjord and Voss

The **Hardangerfjord**, the third-longest fjord in Norway, lies 75km (47 miles) southeast of Bergen. Boat trips can be arranged from Bergen harbour for the length or part of the fjord, or as part of one of the popular Nutshell Tours, which do a **Hardanger in a Nutshell** (www.norwaynutshell.com), taking in the fjord and surrounding areas. There are a number of sights, natural and man-made, alongside or near the fjord and along the smaller fjords connected to it. In the south, **Folgefonn Glacier**, Norway's third-largest ice field, became a national park in 2005. It offers summer skiing, snowboarding and sledding. Nearby, the picturesque town of **Rosendal** has Norway's only baronial mansion, dating from 1665. On the opposite side of the Handangerfjord, heading north, lies **Norheimsund**, worth a visit for its grand old hotel, as well as its scenic location. Hotel Sandven is more than 150 years old and has been beautifully restored over 15 years by Tron Bach, who spent a small fortune returning it to its former glory. The hotel is packed with antique furniture and had splendid views over the fjord and town – the latter seems to have sprung up almost entirely around the hotel, which was built with royal consent. The café and bar are open to non-guests. The hotel is surrounded by historic buildings and even has a mini-museum of old carriages in what used to be the court house *(see Accommodation, page 137)*.

The area between Norheimsund and Bergen, following highway No. 7, **Tveitakvitingen**, is well known for cross-country skiing in winter, and many chalets dot the landscape.

Further inland along the fjord, in the village of Utne, the **Hardanger Folk Museum** (tel: 53-67 00 40; Mon–Fri 10am–3pm, June–Aug until 5pm; charge) features a medieval log house and general store among other things, and there are traditional Hardanger boats in the boathouse. On the Sørfjorden arm of the main fjord, **Kinsarvik** has one of Norway's first stone churches, dating from around 1250

A helicopter ride over Voss

and nearby **Lofthus** is home to Grieg's hut, which the composer used as a retreat. These days it's part of the garden of Hotel Ullsvang. All three villages can be reached by the regular ferry service plying the Hardangerfjord.

Crossing the fjord and travelling north on Highway 13, you reach the town of **Voss**. It has successfully marketed itself as Norway's adventure sports capital and lives up to the name. Voss has a history dating back to medieval times, with an ancient stone church and a folk museum, but these days the enthusiasts who flock to the town are mostly looking for chills and thrills of the extreme kind. Voss organises an annual extreme sports festival for a week every June (www.visitvoss.no), attracting large numbers of adrenalin junkies. If you're feeling adventurous this is the place to try paragliding, parasailing and bungee-jumping, whitewater rafting, horse riding and a number of winter sports.

Voss is the place to come for adventure sports

CENTRAL NORWAY AND THE WESTERN FJORDS

The central part of Norway has some of the country's most understated, as well as its most spectacular, landscapes. By the Swedish border to the east lie quiet forests and sedate farmlands. Moving west the landscape gradually changes into one of glaciers, high plateaux and lofty mountains, including the country's highest peaks. Finally in the far west the dramatic peaks meet the sea, in what has become Norway's most famous natural scenery, the fjords.

The Central East

The landscape of southeastern Norway is characterised by lakes and forests, reminiscent of the Swedish countryside. The area is rich in history with many fortresses and fortifications going back to the time when Sweden and Norway had less than neighbourly relations. **Kongsvinger**, 110km (68 miles) northeast of Oslo, is dominated by an imposing fortress on a hill overlooking the town, and the so-called Vinger Royal Road running through town was the main route in the early Middle Ages for pilgrims from Sweden on their way to St Olaf the Holy's tomb at Trondheim. **Eidsvoll**, some 70km (43 miles) north of Oslo and west of Kongsvinger, made its name in history when the Norwegians declared independence here in 1814 *(see page 20)*. **Eidsvollbygningen**, the house where it all happened, is now a museum (www.eidsvoll1814.no). Following the E6 highway north of Eidsvoll, the next town of interest is **Hamar**, 66km (41 miles) away. Hamar lies on the shores of Norway's largest lake, **Lake Mjøsa**, and there is a sandy beach right in the town itself. Also on the lake is the world's oldest operating paddle steamer, *Skibladner*, which still runs each summer season. The ruins of Hamar's medieval cathedral, now with a new glass cathedral built over the original ruins, are worth a visit. Nearby **Lillehammer** is known for hosting the 1994 Winter Olympics. You can visit the Norwegian Olympic Museum, and take a chair-lift to the top of the Ski Jumping Arena. If you are not feeling sporty, there is the Maihaugen Open-air Museum of rural life and a good art gallery. Continuing north from Lillehammer along Highway E6 it is some 170km (106 miles) to Norway's oldest national park, **Rondane**, founded in 1962, home to wild reindeer, and encompassing the cross-country skiing Troll Trail. The road passes through the beautiful **Gudbrandsdalen valley** with quaint farmhouses, steeped in history. There is also the chance to try out whitewater rafting on the Sjoa River.

The Mountainous Centre

The rail journey from Oslo to Bergen passes some of central Norway's most varied scenery (*see box below*) on its way across the country. The valley of **Hallingdal**, around 100km

The Oslo to Bergen Railway

The Bergen Line, the highest mainline railway line in northern Europe, runs for 496km (308 miles), between Norway's two main cities. It crosses the Hardangervidda plateau at 1,237m (4,058ft), and the highest station is Fisne at 1,222m (4,008ft). It was originally opened from Bergen to Voss in 1883 and then from Voss to Myrdal in 1907. The line passes some of the most scenic areas in Norway – the Hallingdal valley, the ski resort of Geilo and the Hallingskarvet plateau. The journey takes seven hours in total and the train makes a special stop at the highest station in case anyone should wish to nip out for a photo or some fresh, but nippy, air. The station of Myrdal, about halfway through the journey, is where another famous railway begins – Flåmbanen, which runs from Myrdal at 881m (2,890ft) down to Flåm at sea level.

Norway is a great destination for scenic rail journeys

(62 miles) north of Oslo, is well known for its traditional culture and folk music. At the northern end of the valley, **Gol** has one of Norway's best preserved stave churches, dating from 1216. Fifty km (31 miles) southwest, **Geilo**, between Hemsedalsfjella mountain and the Hallingskarvet plateau, is one of Norway's best downhill ski resorts. For less wintry exercise, the **Navvies' Road** (Rallarvegen), a former works access road during the construction of the Oslo–Bergen railway line, is now one of Norway's most popular cycling routes, starting at **Haugastøl** on scenic Ustevatn, 22km (14 miles) southwest of Geilo. The main stretch runs for 92km (57 miles) from Haugastøl to Flåm. Another way to reach Flåm is via the Flåmbanen railway (www.flaamsbana.no) from Myrdal – one of the most attractive rail journeys in the world *(see box opposite)*. The 20km (12½-mile) hour-long train ride takes in majestic mountains, spectacular waterfalls and deep ravines, before emerging at Flåm on the

Hardangervidda is perfect for camping in summer

Aurlandsfjord. Work began on the line in 1923 and took almost 20 years to complete. Today it is mostly a tourist route, with guiding in several languages and occasional photo stops. On Highway No. 7, designated as a National Tourist Route, travelling southwest from Haugastøl, you reach **Hardangervidda National Park** (Nasjonalpark), Norway's largest, covering 3,422 sq km (1,321 sq miles). The vast area is popular for hiking and fishing in summer or cross-country skiing in winter, and there are numerous overnight shelters within the park. Hardangervidda has some of the world's largest wild reindeer herds roaming free, and there is plenty of other wildlife and birdlife to enjoy. The **Hardanger Nature Centre** (tel: 53-67 40 00; www.hardangervidda.org; daily Apr–Oct 10am–6pm, mid-June–mid-Aug until 8pm, Nov–Mar by appointment only) off route 7 near Eidfjord, has lots of information about the park, a good restaurant and can organise tours.

Also near Eidfjord, **Vøringsfossen Waterfall** is one of the most splendid waterfalls in Norway, dropping 182m (597ft), of which 145m (476ft) is a sheer drop straight down into Måbødalen valley below. The hotel near the fall does great hot chocolate and cakes. **Eidfjord** itself, at the end of the fjord of the same name, an arm of the great Hardangerfjord, has become a popular centre for different outdoor activities including adventure sports and ice climbing in winter (www.visiteidfjord.no). The Eidfjord branches out into another arm, home to the small community of **Ulvik**, perched on the waterfront. It's worth having a look at the old church with original rose paintings from the area, as well as a 12th-century oil painting. The fabulous **Brakanes Hotel** on the waterfront *(see Accommodation, page 137)* is good for an evening drink on the terrace and there is plenty to see and do in the area (www.visitulvik.com).

For those really wanting to go back to nature, the **Hardanger Basecamp** (www.hardangerbasecamp.com) at Osa, a 15-minute drive from Ulvik, does Stone Age living and survival courses, and serves great waffles in the café. The Hardanger area is famous for apples, which have been grown there for centuries, and four apple-growing farms have banded together to create the **Hardanger Saft- og Siderfabrikk** (tel: 56-52 61 61; www.hardangersider.no) producing juice, cider and apple brandy. The factory organises pre-booked guided tours with tastings and information about the production process, and there is a restaurant with lovely views.

Scenic routes

The Norwegian tourist board has designated six different routes as national tourist routes – roads that pass through some of the best scenery in Norway. These include: Lofoten, Helgeland, Rondane, Old Strynefjell, Sognefjell and Hardanger tourist routes (www.visitnorway.com).

The Western Fjords

Taking in the beauty of the Nærøyfjord from a tour boat

Travelling north from Ulvik, the **Sognefjord** is the largest fjord in Norway and the second longest in the world, branching out into a number of arms, such as **Aurlandsfjord**, with the little community of **Aurlandsvangen**. The scenery here on a sunny summer day goes beyond the breathtaking. None of the scenic fjord communities has more than 300–400 permanent inhabitants, but in summer they swell enormously with visitors coming to enjoy the landscape. For the best views, drive to the **Stegastein lookout**, above Aurlandsvangen, a wood and glass structure with a sheer drop and a vertigo-inducing view. Norway's most recent addition to the Unesco list, the **Nærøyfjord**, the country's narrowest, can also be visited on a tour boat or regular ferry to Gudvangen. Undredal, en route to Gudvangen, has an excellent stave church. The main road from Aurlandsvangen to Lærdal passes through the Lærdal tunnel, the longest road tunnel in the world at 24.5km (15 miles), another tremendous feat of Norwegian engineering. Just after the tunnel, route 37 leads off to **Borgund**, which has a famous stave church *(see box page 19)*. Continuing across another arm of the Sognefjord, the **Årdalsfjord**, you come to **Sogndal**, the main hub of the Sognefjord.

cathedral. Trondheim has a great mixture of old and new buildings as many successive fires have ravished the city, the one in 1651 destroying 90 percent of the buildings.

The centre of Trondheim is best explored on foot. The main square, **Torget**, is a good place from which to set off, as it is also where you find the tourist information office (www.trondeheim.no). Also in the main square is one of Trondheim's newest shopping complexes, Trondheim Torg, with 75 shops to choose from. It is worth a visit not just for the retail opportunities, but for the unusual architecture, as some of the old wooden buildings have been incorporated into the new mall.

A five-minute walk takes you up to Trondheim's main sight, the **Nidaros Cathedral** (Nidarosdomen; tel: 73-89 08 00; www.nidarosdomen.no; times vary; charge), at Bispegata 5, the northernmost cathedral in the world and the largest in Scandinavia. The cathedral dates back to 1070, when it was built on the site of St Olaf the Holy's tomb, but has been much rebuilt over the centuries. The stunning stained glass is mostly from the early 20th century. During the Middle Ages the cathedral was part of the main European pilgrims' route, with many flocking to the site of St Olaf's tomb. In recent years the old pilgrims' route has been revived, with the Oslo–Trondheim stretch reopened in 1997. In 2010 St Olaf's Way was declared a European Cultural Route by the Council of Europe. The Nidaros Pilgrim Centre behind the cathedral can supply information (www. pilegrimsgarden.no). Next to

Trondheim

the cathedral are two of the city's best museums, the **Archbishop's Palace** (Erkebisgarden) and the **Army Museum** (Rustkammeret), both housed in the oldest secular building in Scandinavia. The former displays crowns and sceptres and other regal items; the latter concentrates on World War II and the Resistance.

The area around the cathedral is jokingly known as the Hallelujah Quarter, since it also contains an Evangelical church, a Catholic church and a Jewish synagogue, all in close proximity. Walking through the park behind the cathedral and following the river past the Pilgrims' Centre, you reach the **Old Town Bridge** (Gamle Bybro) and the old town gates. There has been a bridge to the east river bank since 1681, but the current one dates from 1861. The east side of the Nidelva River is known as **Bakklandet**, where former workers' dwellings and old wharves have been turned into quirky shops

The popular islet of Munkholmen

and eateries. The views over the river and the colourfully painted buildings are particularly good from the bridge at sunset.

Crossing back to Midtbyen you come to the **Church of Our Lady** (Vår Frues Kirke; open 24 hours; free), Trondheim's second medieval church. Turning back towards the main square, at Munkegata 19,

The Church of Our Lady

lies **Stiftsgarden**, the royal residence, where the royal family stays when in the area (June–Aug Mon–Sat 10am–5pm, Sun noon–5pm; closed during royal visits; charge).

Beyond Midtbyen

There are a number of interesting sights outside Midtbyen itself, not least several fortresses, built at a time when fortifications were necessary to protect it from its belligerent neighbour Sweden. **Munkholmen** is a small island in the Trondheimsfjord, where Benedictine monks built a monastery in the 11th century. By the mid-17th century the monks were gone and it had been turned into a prison and fortress. These days it's a popular recreational area and ferries run from Ravnkloa in Midtbyen from mid-May to mid-Sept (www.trippsbatservice.no).

Another fortress, **Kristiansten Fort** (Kristiansten Festning; tel: 73-80 76 60 for guided tours; daily from 9am until the flag is lowered in the evening), built in 1681 on a hill to the east overlooking Trondheim, has great views across town and the surrounding fjord landscape. The road here runs past the University of Science and Technology, opened in 1910.

The Rockheim museum is dedicated to popular music

A recently developed shopping area with plenty of restaurants and nightlife to choose from is **Solsiden** on the east side of Nidelva. The harbour area in general is being opened up and developed throughout and this is also home to recently opened **Rockheim** (Brattørkaia 14; tel: 73-60 50 70; www.rockheim.no), a museum housed in an eye-catching modern building just north of Trondheim's central train station and dedicated to pop and rock music.

Take the Stavset bus No. 8 from Trondheim city centre to visit **Sverresborg Trøndelag Folk Museum** (Sverresborg Allé 13; tel: 73-89 01 05; www.sverresborg.no; June–Aug daily 11am–6pm, Sept–May Mon–Fri 11am–3pm, Sat–Sun noon–4pm; charge), one of Norway's largest open-air museums, set around the ruins of a medieval castle. More than 60 buildings include one of the oldest stave churches in the country, dating from 1170, along with Sami huts and 18th-century town houses.

Other Trøndelag Attractions

Don't be taken aback if the tourist board in Trondheim asks you if you would like to go to Hell. **Hell** is only half an hour's drive from central Trondheim and it's become a bit of a tourist attraction because of its name. If having your photo taken in front of the railway station of Hell is your cup of tea, this is the place for you. Somewhere of more interest and historical significance is **Stiklestad** some 90km (56 miles) northeast, where Olaf the Holy fell in battle in 1030. It has 30 historic buildings dating back to the 17th century, a medieval farm and holds an annual St Olaf festival in July (www.stiklestad.no).

   Further to the south of Trondheim, the Unesco World Heritage town of **Røros** should not be missed. An old mining town near the Swedish border, it was founded more than 300 years ago and it has an unusually large collection of 100 perfectly preserved wooden houses from the 18th century. A

Unesco World Heritage Sites

Since 1979 eight different parts of Norway's natural and cultural heritage have made it onto the Unesco list of World Heritage Sites. Some, such as the Geiranger fjord and the old quarter of Bergen, are well known, whereas others have not yet become so renowned. The first two to be added were Bryggen, the medieval Hanseatic area of central Bergen, and Urnes stave church, in 1979. This was followed by the mining town of Røros near the Swedish border in south Trøndelag in 1980 and the rock paintings at Alta in Finnmark in 1985. Almost 20 years went by before Unesco turned its attention towards Norway again when in 2004 the Vegaøyan Archipelago was listed, as well as the Struve Geodetic Arc in 2005. The latter is shared with a number of other countries. That same year the western fjords were also recognised, and the Geiranger and Nærøyfjord now also have Unesco status.

walking tour of Røros will take in the majority of the sights and it is also possible to visit the Olavsgruva Mine with three centuries of mining history (www.roros.no; *see box on page 65*). The very southernmost part of Trøndelag is home to **Dovrefjell-Sunndalsfjella National Park**, the only place in Norway where you can see the impressive musk ox.

The coastal landscape of Trøndelag is dotted with islands and skerries, somewhat understated and flatter than the fjords further south. Here tiny, quaint cottages and isolated settlements hug the seashore, some only reached by boat. This is an area perfect for cycling, fishing or island hopping (www.trondelag.com has more information).

Nordland

Travelling north from Trondheim into the next county, Nordland, you will reach the town of **Mo i Rana**, known for its ironworks, near which lies the **Svartisen-Saltfjellet National Park**. The second-largest glacier in Norway, Svartisen is popular for glacier walks in summer. Continuing north you will come to **Saltstraumen**, 33km (20 miles) south of Bodø, where you can experience the strongest maelstrom, or whirlpool current, in the world. The speed of the water rushing through the narrow inlet between the Saltfjord and the Skjerstadfjord has been recorded at over 20 knots. Between June and August there are daily boat trips to get you closer to the tidal currents and to the birdlife – the rare sea eagle can be spotted here (www.saltstraumen-adventure.com).

Bodø, the administrative centre of Nordland, has fewer than 50,000 inhabitants. It's very manageable in size, and with Norway's northernmost railway linking it to the rest of the country it's become a gateway to the region and the nearby Lofoten Islands. On the surface, the centre of Bodø may not have that much to offer, although it is beautifully situated between two fjords, the Saltfjord and the Landegodefjord. The city was heavily bombed during World War II and few buildings survived the onslaught, but the area around the harbour is picturesque and nice for a stroll. One of Bodø's main sights is the **Norwegian Aviation Museum** (Norsk Luftfartsmuseum; www.luftfart.museum.no; Mon–Fri 10am–5pm, Sat–Sun 11am–4pm; charge), in a building shaped like a giant propeller, close to Bodø airport. It includes civil and military aviation history sections. Nearby Bodøsjøen, on the Saltfjord, has an open-air museum and a beach for the hardy outdoor enthusiast – temperatures rarely rise above 14°C (57°F).

Half an hour north of Bodø by car and ferry lies the scenic old trading post of **Kjerringøy**, and the whole area is good for hiking. Most of Nordland lies above the Arctic Circle, making this a good area to see the midnight sun in summer and northern lights in autumn and winter.

Svartisen is Norway's second-largest glacier

Lofoten Islands and Narvik

Svolvær is the main town on the Lofoten islands

From Bodø it's a four-hour boat journey to the port of **Stamsund**, on the remote and beautiful **Lofoten Islands**. The archipelago has six main islands and has been inhabited since Viking times. It has a 1,000-year history of cod fishing, and to this day Norway's most authentic fishing culture can be found here. Stamsund, on Vestvågøy in southern Lofoten, is a quiet old village where many of the old fishermen's cabins, *rorbuer,* have been converted into accommodation for visitors. These cabins date from the time when large numbers of fishermen would come across from the mainland for the annual cod fishing season. Stamsund is also renowned for its puppet theatre festival, and there are no less than three theatres in this village of only 1,400 people.

The road leading south from Stamsund and Leknes passes some of the islands' most stunning scenery – misty high peaks rising sharply from the water's edge, and the water itself, a dark turquoise with improbably white sandy beaches. Set amid this grandeur of nature is the **Lofotr Viking Museum** in Borg (www.lofotr.no; May–Aug daily 10am–4pm, Sept–Apr Sun only 1–3pm; charge), which also holds Viking feasts in summer. Continuing south, you reach the islands of Flakstadøya and Moskenesøya, the former with spectacular scenery and good accommodation possibilities in Flakstad and Ramberg. The latter is a haven for artists, particularly around **Reine**, which is also an arts and crafts centre. Reaching the southernmost tip of the island, make a stop at the oddly named little town of **Å**. This tiny community has two of the islands' best museums, offering better insights into island life and the history of Lofoten. The **Norwegian Fishing Village Museum** (Norsk Fiskevaermuseum; June–Aug daily 10am–5.30pm, Sept–May Mon–Fri 11am–3.30pm; charge), detailing life in the fishing community over the past 200 years; and the **Stockfish Museum** (Lofoten Tørrfiskmuseum; June–Aug daily 10am–5.30pm, Sept–May limited hours; charge), with displays and lively information on the processing and export of stockfish – a lot more interesting than it sounds. Å itself is appealing, with a quaint, old-world feel and a number of red-painted *rorbuer*.

Svolvær, on the island of Austvågøya, is the main town on the islands, with a pleasant harbour and a number of older buildings. From here there are popular tours of scenic **Trollfjorden**, a 40-minute boat trip away and surrounded by sheer cliffs with magnificent waterfalls. Nearby **Henningsvær** is a centre for rock climbing and unusual craft- and clothes shops (www.lofoten.info for information about the islands).

When the LoFast Road opened in December 2007, the Lofoten Islands were finally connected to the mainland, cutting journey times and making it a lot easier to get around.

Private cell

An old shop in Å in Lofoten is one of the few places in Norway to have a private prison cell in the basement, hailing from a time when the lord of the manor had the powers to lock up the unruly who had been celebrating the end of the fishing season too hard.

12 ➤   **Narvik**, the last main town in Nordland before reaching Tromsø, is situated on the Ofotenfjord near the Swedish border. It is worth a visit mainly for its interesting World War II history. One of the fiercest battles in Norway between British and German destroyers was fought here in the fjord in April 1940, and the **War Memorial Museum** (www.destination narvik.com) tells the story. Next door to the museum is a small fish market with an accompanying restaurant. Narvik is also known for its railway, built at the turn of the 20th century to connect it with the mines in Swedish Lapland, since Narvik has an ice-free port year-round, thanks to the Gulf Stream.

War monuments commemorate the 1940 Battle of Narvik

THE FAR NORTH

Troms and Finnmark are the two northernmost counties of Norway, the latter reaching as far as the Russian border to the east. Both counties are situated above the Arctic Circle. Tromsø is the main city in Troms, whereas Alta has the highest population in Finnmark, although Vadsø is the capital. The far north is a sparsely populated area of outstanding natural beauty. It is also the traditional home of the Sami people, and Sami culture is particularly centred around the towns of Karasjok and Kautokeino.

Tromsø

13 The city centre of **Tromsø** is situated on the island of Tromsøya. The main road from the south crosses the 1km (½-mile) Tromsø Bridge, an imposing structure that blends nicely with the landscape and links the island to the mainland. The Hurtigruten terminal, bus station and tourist inform-ation office can all be found in the same place, near the

Bust of Roald Amundsen at the Polar Museum

quayside at Prostneset. This is a good place to start exploring the sights of the city. Tromsø centre is nice and easy to get around and has a surprisingly large number of old wooden buildings that have survived the ravages of World War II.

Following the quayside you get to the **Polar Museum** (Polarmuseet; tel: 77-60 66 30; www.polarmuseum.no; daily from 11am, closing times vary; charge) at Søndre Tollbodgate 11, which opened in 1978, 50 years to the day after Roald Amundsen set off from the city on his last expedition. Housed in an old customs house, the museum depicts Amundsen's journeys, exhibits some of his paintings and has a wealth of information on the history of Arctic trappers and more. Be aware that the displays of seal clubbing are graphic and may upset some people.

From the museum follow Bispegata to the start of Storgata, one of the main streets and home to **Perspektivet Museum,** housed in a neoclassical manor house and focusing on Tromsø's past and present. A few doors down, the Verdensteatret theatre is one of the oldest in Norway and has the original decor in the movie salon. The theatre organises

The stunning Arctic Cathedral

a silent film festival every September. Further along Storgata is the main square, Stortorget, and a Catholic church. Further still is the Lutheran cathedral, and continuing right through the centre of Tromsø you reach the **Mack Ølhallen** (Mack Brewery; Mon–Fri 9am–6pm, Sat 9am–3pm, guided tours available; charge), the northernmost brewery in the world ('Mack' is somewhat unfortunately pronounced 'muck'). There is also a beer hall, full of kitsch, including a life-size stuffed polar bear by the entrance.

Just past the Ølhallen lies the Tromsø Gallery of Contemporary Art, and then, down by the waterfront, at Hjalmar Johansensgaten 12, is **Polaria** (Polar Research Centre; tel: 77-75 01 00; www.polaria.no; daily mid-May–Aug 10am–7pm, Sept–mid-May noon–5pm; charge). Don't miss the feeding of the seals daily at 12.30pm in summer.

Across the bridge in Tromsdalen, the **Arctic Cathedral**, (Ishavskatedralen) built in 1965, is an unusual and daring structure in stark white, and in the shape of a massive triangle. It is open year-round, and in summer there are late-night concerts to coincide with the midnight sun.

Tromsø to the North Cape

North of Tromsø, the **Lyngen Alps** (Lyngenalpene) mountain range, bordered by the Lyngen fjord on one side and the Ullsfjord on the other, is an area of high peaks, reminiscent of the Alps. The highest summit reaches 1,833m (6,014ft) and several glaciers can be found here. This remote region has a good mountain lodge open year-round, the Lyngen Lodge (www.lyngenlodge.com).

Crossing into **Finnmark**, Norway's northernmost county, **Alta**, with some 17,000 people, is the main population and administrative centre. Perhaps surprisingly for such a remote place, Alta is on the Unesco list of World Heritage Sites *(see page 65)*. On the southern outskirts of Alta, at Hjemmeluft, as many as 5,000 rock carvings were discovered in 1972, dating back over 6,000 years. The carvings can be visited at the **World Heritage Centre for Rock Art – Alta Museum** (www.alta.museum.no; late June–late Aug daily 8am–8pm, reduced hours out of season; charge).

Rock carvings at Alta

Further north along the coast is **Hammerfest**, which prides itself on being the northernmost city in the world, although with only 9,000 inhabitants this might be stretching the definition of 'city'. However, by Norwegian law you only have to have more than 5,000 inhabitants to qualify. **Hon-**

ningsvåg, further north still, is in dispute with Hammerfest as to which is the northernmost city, but Honningsvåg has the advantage of attracting the tourists as a gateway to the **⑮** ➤ **North Cape** (Nordkapp), on Magerøya island. Although not strictly speaking the very northernmost point of mainland Europe, since it's on an island, it is now renowned as such and pulls in the visitors accordingly. The journey across Magerøya to the North Cape takes under an hour and the landscape is starkly beautiful and barren. Honningsvåg is the main hub, but there are another four fishing hamlets on the island, three on the east coast and one on the west.

The North Cape itself, at latitude 71° north, has a large, modern visitors' centre, looking somewhat out of place in this landscape of natural beauty (www.nordkapp.no; mid-May–Aug 11am–1pm, early May and Sept 11am–3pm, Oct–Apr 12.30–2pm, to coincide with buses). The cliff plunges 307m (1,007ft) into the Barents Sea below, but it's not just the cape itself that is worth a visit. The scenery surrounding it is quite remarkable – barren at first glance, but home to some 205 different plant species.

In the Finnmark interior, **Karasjok** and **Kautokeino** are Norway's main centres for Sami culture, although all of Finnmark and several other counties have Sami communities. In Karasjok around 90 percent of the population speak Sami as a first language, and the area is home to more than 60,000 reindeer. Both towns are good places to find out more about Sami culture and traditions, and there are several cultural centres, including the **Sami Collections** (www.rdm.no) in Karasjok, an open-air museum. For more information

Arctic Ski Pass

The Arctic Ski Pass is valid at four ski resorts in northern Sweden and Norway, including the ski slopes outside Narvik. See www.narvikfjellet.com for more information.

A polar bear roams Svalbard's Arctic wilderness

other activities. In some parts of the islands these winter activities are offered all year round, as 63 percent of Svalbard is covered by glaciers and the snow never goes away. Bear in mind that this is an Arctic wilderness and a fragile environment. Svalbard tourism council has more information and guidelines for visitors, as well as a handy list of tour operators for all the activities on offer (tel: 79-02 55 50; www.svalbard.net; Svalbard Reiseliv, Longyearbyen).

Jan Mayen

This volcanic island, lying between Greenland and Norway, is the country's furthest outpost. There are no commercial flights and no natural harbours. To visit you need to obtain a permit from the Norwegian government. Independent travel is not possible but an organisation called EcoExpeditions arranges trips by sailing boat (www.eco expeditions.no).

WHAT TO DO

Norway, although mainly known for its natural wonders, also has a rich and varied history and cultural life. In summer there are many events that combine nature and culture, with festivals and concerts held outdoors in scenic settings. Winter offers an increasing range of options from first-rate skiing and other winter sports, to Christmas markets and the spectacular phenomenon of the northern lights.

SPORTS AND OUTDOOR PURSUITS

Summer

Hiking and glacier walking. Nothing is a more popular Norwegian pastime than to '*gå på tur*' – something that involves strapping on a good pair of boots, taking a packed lunch and spending a day hiking amid some of the glorious scenery, be it mountain, fjord, forest or field *(see box on page 85)*. There are countless hiking trails, and good-quality maps can usually be obtained from local tourist offices. Some of Norway's many national parks – 33 on the mainland, seven on Svalbard – such as Jotunheimen or Hardangervidda are good bets, and the majority of trails are well kept and clearly marked with cairns or signposts. If you are planning to hike, bear in mind that the season only runs from May to October and in the far north it's even shorter. The weather can be very changeable even in the height of summer, so take local advice before setting out. The Norwegian Trekking Association has further information and organises tours (www.turistforeningen.no). The short summer season is also a good time to try out glacier walking. Nigardsbreen, an arm

Norway is a hiker's paradise

A rural bike ride at Oslofjord

of Jostedalsbreen glacier, allows the adventurous to explore the glacier, with an experienced guide, on two-to five-hour blue ice walks, from mid-June to the middle of September (www.joste dal.com). Glacier walking on Okstindan and Svartisen in the Arctic Circle can also be arranged. Check Rana Spesialsport (www.spesial sport.no).

Cycling. Norwegian roads are comparatively quiet, making them excellent for cycling in spring, summer and autumn. City roads tend to have cycle paths and in the countryside traffic is rarely a problem. It's easy to rent bikes, even in rural areas, where hotels and guesthouses often rent them out by the hour or by the day. In mountainous areas cycling can be challenging and also bear in mind that distances can be great, with facilities few and far between, especially in the far north. The Navvies' Road (Rallarvegen) is one of the most popular routes, running from Haugastøl or Finse, to Flåm or Voss, 108km (67 miles) at its longest. Another popular option is the North Sea Cycle Route, part of the world's longest biking route, passing through seven countries. Bike Norway can give you further information and supply route maps (www.bike-norway.com).

Fishing. In a country blessed with so much water, it is no surprise that fishing is ever-popular. It is possible to go deep-sea fishing, freshwater fishing or salmon fishing. The Lofoten Islands have some of the best waters and arguably the most authentic fishing culture, with their old fishermen's cabins, *rorbuer*, many of which offer accommodation. There are organised fishing tours in many parts of Norway (check with local tourist offices) or you can get a national fishing licence, available to purchase online from www.inatur.no.

Climbing. Mountaineering is a popular sport in many areas. Lofoten, with its stark, forbidding mountains, is a centre for rock climbing, with a climbing school in Henningsvær (www.nordnorskklatreskole.no). Other areas include Jotunheimen, where the peaks reach 2,000m (over 6,000ft), Vesterålen Mountains and the Lyngen Alps. You could also try ice climbing – climbing up frozen waterfalls – in Rjukan. The Norwegian Trekking Association, DNT, runs mountain-climbing courses (www.turistforeningen.no).

Rafting, sailing and canoeing. Rafting can be done both on the many rivers and at sea. Deep-sea rafting on the Vestfjord

Sailing is a popular pastime in Norway

The midnight sun is best viewed at sea

between the Lofoten Islands and the mainland is possible if the wind and currents are right. Sailing is popular mainly in southern Norway and on the Oslo fjord. Canoeing and kayaking can be tried pretty much anywhere there is water, but the western fjords are particularly scenic, while the far north is more tranquil, with fewer pleasure boats and ferries. The Norwegian Canoe Association has more information (www.padling.no).

Wildlife and birdwatching. There are ample opportunities to spot wildlife such as reindeer and elk in many parts of Norway, or the more illusive musk oxen in Dovrefjell National Park (www.moskussafari.no), and the giant king crab in Finnmark. Birdlife is abundant with 473 recorded species, inland and along the coastline. For a combination of birdwatching and king crab safaris, Arctic Tourist (www.arctictourist.no) in Finnmark is a good option.

Midnight sun. The midnight sun is visible in many parts of northern Norway from May to August depending on latitude. The best and most unrestricted views are from higher ground or at sea.

Winter

Cross-country and downhill skiing. Skiing is the most popular winter sport in Norway with more than 7,000km (4,350 miles) of cross-country tracks laid out by the DNT (Norwegian Trekking Association) alone. There are even tracks within the Oslo city limits and most municipalities have their own ski tracks, sometimes floodlit in the evenings for after-work exercise. Jotunheimen, Rondane and Dovrefjell national parks have some of the best cross-country skiing in Norway. Alpine or downhill skiing is also an option in various parts of the country, from Geilo, Hemsedal and Trysil in the centre, to Narvik further north. The best time for skiing is February to April, but it's usually possible to ski from November until mid-May. For good up-to-date information on snow conditions, check www.skiinfo.no.

Gå På Tur: **Mastering the Great Outdoors**

To *gå på tur*, literally to 'go on tour', is one of those quintessentially Norwegian concepts that seemingly every Norwegian will indulge in, if not every weekend, then certainly on a regular basis. It involves heading out into the countryside, in warm clothes and sturdy footwear, and hiking through the great outdoors – often in the mountains, but any bit of countryside will do. The day is not complete without the obligatory stop to eat a packed lunch, usually doorstep sandwiches and a thermos of hot, black coffee. On summer weekends, in the many scenic areas of the country, whole families, young and old, venture forth and energetically conquer the peaks and fjordlands from north to south, particularly in the 33 national parks.

Ice-fishing is a fun,
if chilly, activity

Dog-sledding. There are organised dog-sledding trips, mostly in the north of the country, that last for anything from an hour or two up to five-day excursions. You can choose between steering your own sled or sitting snugly wrapped up with your own musher and a team of dogs doing all the hard work. Visit Norway has more information (www.visitnorway.com); or try Nordland Adventures (www.nordlandturselskap.no).

Ice-skating. Come winter a number of outdoor ice rinks open up, such as the popular one in Oslo city centre, near the National Theatre. Then there are the natural ice rinks in the form of frozen lakes, rivers and fjords – but do take local advice before venturing out on these. At the man-made ice rinks, skates can usually be hired and it's sometimes possible to have lessons.

Ice-fishing or *pimpling*. For this sport a hole is simply drilled through the ice, which you can then fish through and get a good catch, even in winter. Bring waterproof gloves and a thermos of hot chocolate. A company called Competent Travels (www.competenttravels.no) organises three-day ice-fishing safaris from Tromsø.

Northern Lights. The Northern Lights, *aurora borealis*, can best be spotted in October, February and March, between 6pm and 1am at night. The best displays of light can be seen above the Arctic Circle, where there is less light pollution, but the northern lights can also be seen further south. Remember to wrap up warm on these excursions.

SHOPPING

Prices can be high for consumer goods, but some 3,000 shops across Norway are participating in a tax-free shopping scheme. Look for the tax-free logo in the windows of participating shops. The sales tax/VAT in Norway is 25 percent on many items and 12–19 percent can be claimed back by visitors from non-EU/EEA countries. The refund can be made through the Global Refund Cash Refund Offices at land border crossings, airports, on board ferries and cruise ships.

The quality of most items is usually very high and some of the handicraft traditions go back hundreds of years. Look for the *salg* sign in windows, indicating a sale or special offers.

Where to Shop

The main cities of Oslo, Bergen, Stavanger and Trondheim all have good shopping areas, and some of Norway's smaller towns also have interesting shops, particularly for handicrafts. Oslo has everything from department stores such as Glasmagasinet and House of Oslo, Norway's largest, to quirky, independent boutiques in the up-and-coming area of Grünerløkka and trendy Majorstuen. Aker Brygge is another good

There are plenty of shopping opportunities in Oslo

Fresh produce at Bergen fish market

shopping area, where the old converted shipyard in the harbour houses shops, restaurants and bars. In Bergen, the area around Bryggen, Strandkaien, Strandgaten and Torget has many small, interesting shops whose goods include handicrafts, furs and knitwear. This is also the area of the famous Fish Market, perfect for buying lunch, fresh fish and seafood.

The Stavanger region is particularly good for glass, and you can visit glass-blowing studios and buy the products in speciality craft shops. The centre of Trondheim, Midtbyen, has both traditional and modern shopping opportunities: the Trondheim Torg mall, with 75 stores, plus cafés and restaurants, recently opened near the main square, and more old-fashioned shops can be found in Jomfrugaten (Maiden Street), where most of the businesses are run by women. There are plenty of other shopping options in Norway. Tromsø, for example, has numerous shops and boutiques housed in old, wooden buildings; and in the far north there are excellent Sami handicrafts (called *duodji*), such as silverware and items made from reindeer hide or bone.

What to Buy

This is just a small selection of recommended things to buy that are either unique to Norway or particularly good value.

Handicrafts. The craft traditions in Norway go back many hundred years and the roots of today's modern designs, using locally available materials, can be found in the old crafts. Knitwear, such as sweaters, scarves, gloves, mittens and hats, is internationally renowned, as it is of excellent quality. Woodcraft, glassware, silverware and jewellery, reindeer pelts and weavings are other popular items to take home. In the far north, as mentioned above, there are interesting Sami handicrafts for sale.

Local food and drink. Norway has a number of locally produced specialities, ranging from smoked salmon and stockfish *(tørrfisk)* to akvavit, and Mack beer from the world's northernmost brewery in Tromsø. Reindeer and elk salamis and cloudberry jams are other products to take home if you want to relive a taste of Norway.

Clothes. Men's and women's clothes are often nicely designed, but can be expensive. Knitwear features heavily, but there are also plenty of lighter items and summer clothing. As a rule there are more individual shops than chains, although international brands are quite common in the main cities. Norwegian designer shop Moods of Norway has made it big in Japan and Beverly Hills with its colourful designs (www.moodsofnorway.com).

Sports and outdoor gear. Norwegians are quite possibly the sportiest people in the world and this is reflected in their shops. Excellent all-weather outdoor gear and winter clothes can be found across the country, including entire ski outfits, as well as skis and ice-skates.

Oslo's iconic Opera House

ENTERTAINMENT

In a country as large as Norway, with a population of less than five million, the quality and variety of entertainment varies widely from region to region and, of course, between city and countryside. There is a long-standing musical and theatrical tradition in Norway, with a number of festivals celebrating both these art forms, particularly during the summer months. Tickets for events in Norway can be booked in advance via the Norwegian branch of Ticketmaster (tel: 81-53 31 33; www.billettservice.no). Tourist offices are sometimes able to help out with booking events and concerts.

Music, Opera and Dance

Classical music is alive and well in Norway, celebrating national composers such as Edvard Grieg. The **Oslo Philharmonic Orchestra** has an excellent reputation, and its home base is at the city's **Konserthus**; the season starts at the end of August and runs until early June (check www.oslofilharmonien.no for concert schedules and tickets). **Bergen Philharmonic Orchestra** is based at **Grieghallen** (www.harmonien.no); and there is also the **Norwegian Arctic Philharmonic Orchestra**, founded in 2009 and based in **Tromsø** (www.noso.no).

Jazz is very big in Norway *(see Calendar of Events, page 95)*, and while the classical music season runs from autumn to spring, jazz festivals and venues kick off in summer. There are well over 30 jazz venues across the country, including some that are off the beaten track. For more information see www.jazz-clubs-worldwide.com. In recent years there has been a rise in so-called Black Metal rock music and this genre is one of Norway's greatest musical exports. Traditional Norwegian folk music remains popular, and since Alexander Rybak won the Eurovision Song Contest in 2009, the Halling folk dance and fiddle-playing, used in the winning song, have increased in popularity even more. The dance hails from Hallingdal valley, in the Buskerud district.

Oslo has a brand-new **Opera House**, which opened in 2008, right on the harbour. It is home to the national opera and the national ballet (www.operaen.no for programme information). This is Norway's first opera house, a stunning building with excellent acoustics, and it has an extensive programme of international operas, concerts and ballets, as well as a festival of chamber music every August.

All that jazz in Norway

Theatre and Cinema

Norway has a proud theatrical tradition, dating back to the late 19th-century works of **Henrik Ibsen** and **Bjørnstjerne Bjørnson**. The **National Theatre** in Oslo (www.national theatret.no), **Den Nationale Scene** in Bergen (www.dns.no), **Rogaland Teater** in Stavanger (www.rogaland-teater.no) and **Trøndelag Teater** in Trondheim (www.trondelag-teater.no) all have extensive programmes, but, naturally, most plays and shows tend to be in Norwegian. At the cinema, on the other hand, films are almost exclusively shown in their original language, with Norwegian subtitles.

Nightlife

The cities of **Oslo**, **Bergen**, **Stavanger** and **Trondheim** all have a busy nightlife, with bars and clubs often staying open until the small hours all year round. In summer, areas such as **Aker Brygge** in Oslo are packed with people enjoying alfresco meals and drinks in the evening. Bars usually shut around 1am or later at the weekend. Bear in mind that the very high cost of alcohol can make a night out expensive, but some places have a happy hour for after-work or early-evening drinks.

In rural areas nightlife is a lot more limited in scope, but there is usually at least one local bar, which can be an interesting experience to visit, since this is where local people congregate. Many of the smaller **fjord communities** are busy in summer and hotels or guesthouses often have bars that are open to the public, as well as to guests. Similarly, **ski resorts** tend to have a good nightlife in winter. The Oslo tourist board at www.visitoslo.com has a useful 'What's on in Oslo' guide.

Adults only

For entry to nightclubs the minimum age can be fairly high, often 21 or above, so remember to bring ID if look younger than you are.

ACTIVITIES FOR CHILDREN

Norway is a very child-friendly nation. Public transport not only has pram access, but buses have special seats that convert to child seats for longer journeys. Most restaurants and cafés have highchairs and offer children's menus. It is not unusual for hotels, campsites and other accommodation to have play areas for little ones and sometimes children's pools. Towns and municipalities have outdoor playgrounds and many public facilities have dedicated play areas. Children often get substantial discounts on

Amusement parks are bound to keep little ones happy

entry fees to sights, at ski centres and on public transport. For many attractions there are also family tickets available.

Cities aren't always the best places for children, but Oslo has numerous ways to keep them entertained and occupied, such as the many museums with interactive areas (www.visitoslo.com). Just 20km (12½ miles) outside Oslo lies **TusenFryd Amusement Park** (late Apr–early Oct times vary; charge), with lots of rides, including Europe's first 5D attraction and a water park. Fifteen km (9 miles) north of Lillehammer, **Hunderfossen Family Park** (www.hunderfossen.no; times vary; charge) has some 50 attractions including a troll park, a high rope course, rafting and a full-scale fairy-tale palace. In winter months it turns into a Winter Park. **Bø Sommarland** (www.sommarland.no; June–Aug; charge), in Telemark, 80km (50 miles) west of Oslo, is Scandinavia's largest water park, with 20 different pools and slides. They also have a Tarzan track, clown shows, canoeing and Europe's only water roller-coaster, the Master Blaster, among other attractions. **Kristiansand Zoo**, just outside Kristiansand, is open year-round, with wildlife from all over the world in five separate parks, including a Children's Farm and an area where you can explore the Nordic wilderness. The zoo also has pirate ships and a games area (www.dyreparken.no).

Norway is a very child-friendly nation

Rockheim in Trondheim (www.rockheim.no; Tue–Sun 11am–6pm; charge), which opened in 2010, is the national interactive experience centre for all things related to Norwegian rock and pop. It's an excellent place to drop off your grumpy teenagers for the afternoon.

Sporting activities are also very child-friendly, and it's usually possible to rent sports equipment such as skis and ice-skates for children, even for toddlers. Norwegian children start skiing, skating and joining their parents for hikes from a very young age and there are good sports instructors for youngsters of all ages.

Calendar of Events

January Northern Lights Festival (Tromsø).

February Opera Festival (Kristiansund).

March Holmenkollen Ski Festival (Oslo). Winter Festival (Narvik), includes sports events, concerts and carnival. The Birkebeiner Race (Rena to Lillehammer), a 53km (33-mile) cross-country ski race, with up to 12,000 participants.

April Jazz festival (Voss), three days of jazz and folk.

May International Festival (Bergen), one of the largest musical events in Scandinavia.

June North Cape March (Honningsvåg), a 68km (42-mile) trek from Honningsvåg to North Cape. Emigration festival (Stavanger and Kvinesdal), commemorating the many Norwegians who emigrated to North America. Midsummer (nationwide), celebrating the summer solstice. Midnight Sun Marathon (Tromsø), northern Norway marathon starting at midnight.

July International Jazz Festival (Kongsberg), open-air concerts and international jazz artists. Bislett Games (Oslo), international athletics competition. International Jazz Festival (Molde), the oldest jazz festival in Norway, held over six days. Olsok festival (Trondheim), commemorating St Olaf the Holy; and the Oi food festival (Trondheim). Gladmat festival (Stavanger), celebrating all things foodie.

August Telemark International Folk Music Festival (Bø), folk music and folk dance festival. Peer Gynt Festival (Vinstra), events in honour of Ibsen's fictional character. Jazz Festival (Oslo), which has been running since 1986. Chamber Music Festival (Oslo), chamber music performed at Akershus Castle and Fortress.

September Oslo Marathon (Oslo).

December Christmas markets (Oslo and nationwide). From Advent (beginning of December) onwards at weekends in many parts of Norway, markets sell unusual Christmas gifts, handicrafts and local delicacies. Nobel Peace Prize Ceremony (Oslo), held at Oslo City Hall, 10 December annually.

EATING OUT

Norwegian cuisine has come into its own in recent years with an emphasis on fresh local produce, and the country's fish and seafood are world-famous, from *bacalao* to Arctic prawns and smoked salmon. There is plenty for the adventurous carnivore to sample as well, with reindeer and elk increasingly featuring on many of the best restaurant menus. A new generation of chefs is rediscovering local produce, sometimes sticking solely to traditional recipes, sometimes adding more international flavours.

Rustic Norwegian home-cooking was traditionally based around what produce was available locally, depending on the changing seasons. Many dishes popular to this day have their roots in the farming or fishing communities from days

Café culture in Bergen

gone by and there is a strong emphasis on fish or game, in the coastal and inland areas respectively. The topography of Norway – coast, farmland, forest, highland and mountains – has meant that different ingredients are popular in different parts of the country. Pickled, dried, smoked, salted and fermented foods all have their origins in the days before refrigeration, preservatives and modern cooking methods, when it was necessary to find alternative ways for storing and preparing foodstuffs that needed to last through the long winters. Some dishes, both fish and meat, have strong flavours and can be a bit of an acquired taste for the uninitiated, but for the most part Norwegian cuisine is fresh, wholesome and tasty, and portions are generous.

This is not to say that you will only find Norwegian food – the cuisine here is increasingly international in flavour. Pizza, pasta and burgers are as common as *lefse*, a round flat-

Food Festivals

Norwegians take their food seriously and over the last decade a number of food festivals have sprung up across the country. *Norsk Matglede* in Geilo, *Gladmat* in Stavanger, the Norwegian Food Festival in Ålesund and *Oi Trøndersk Matfesival* in Trondheim, are just some of the events celebrating all things foodie in Norway. Programmes include everything from tasting sessions to cooking lessons, master chefs' workshops, lectures and special offers from local restaurateurs. Most keep the focus firmly Norwegian, looking into the history and traditions behind modern-day national cuisine, but *Gladmat*, taking over the scenic harbour area of Stavanger every summer, has a more international feel to it. Geilo, at the other end of the spectrum, emphasises small-scale producers and organic food. The festivals are often held in the height of summer, with stalls set up for outdoor sampling and alfresco eating, in some of Norway's loveliest settings.

Fish and seafood can be found on most menus

bread, traditionally made of potato, and *sursild*, pickled herring. A number of international cuisines such as Italian, Chinese, Thai and Indian are well represented, at least in the bigger cities. Also in recent years, a number of annual food festivals, featuring both Norwegian and international cuisine, take place during the summer *(see box page 97)*. Food culture in Norway has numerous regional variations, and what is consumed in Oslo can differ substantially from what is popular in, for example, Bergen or Tromsø, but generally speaking there is an emphasis on using local produce whenever possible. As a rule, in the countryside many of the best restaurants can be found in hotels and guesthouses, which usually serve food to non-guests as well as to residents.

When to Eat

People tend to eat comparatively early in Norway. Despite the majority of Norwegians working away from the home, dinner is still consumed surprisingly early, perhaps harking back to a different era. It is not unusual for restaurants to start serving dinner from 5pm, and in smaller towns it can be difficult to get a meal after 9 or 10pm, when all but a few bars will be closing.

What to Eat

Most hotels serve an international-style breakfast, but for Norwegians breakfast can be anything from hail and hearty to a quick cup of coffee, always taken black. For the working Norwegian the packed lunch, *matpakke*, still reigns supreme, even though eating out or buying a sandwich is becoming more common.

As you would expect, Norwegians eat more fish than people in many other countries, and fish has been a staple of their diet for many centuries. Seafood, on the other hand, is more of a recent addition to the diet.

There are more than 200 species of fish and shellfish in Norwegian waters, some wild, some farmed. Norway is one of the world's largest exporters, sending around 3 million tonnes of its sea harvest to consumers abroad. Some of the most common fish to be found on menus and in markets are cod, salmon, trout, herring, Arctic char, pollack, monkfish, mackerel and redfish. And as if that wasn't enough variety, there is also plaice, turbot, coley, ling, tusk, whiting, haddock, catfish, halibut and flounder to choose from – and these are just the most common species.

Fish is prepared in all sorts of ways, but Norwegian cooking is quite light on spices and seasoning – salt, pepper and a few different herbs, such as dill or mustard seeds, are most frequently used. Boiling, braising, poaching, smoking and pickling are popular ways of preparing fish, often served simply with boiled new potatoes and a bit of butter. Best known of all is probably the Norwegian salmon dish

Christmas flavours

Christmas is the time to try lutefish, mutton rib, ptarmigan and of course beverages of the alcoholic kind – *gløgg* (similar to mulled wine, often spiked with a stronger spirit), *julaøl* (Christmas beer) and, strongest of all, akvavit.

known as *gravlaks*, literally meaning 'buried salmon', a form of curing the fish with salt and sugar. Fish soups, usually milk-based, feature heavily along Norway's coastline, containing a variety of fish and seafood, as well as vegetables and potatoes. Herrings, pickled with all sorts of tasty additions from mustard and onion to tomato and herbs, are another trusty favourite. Fermented trout, *rakfisk*, is a dish that is something of an acquired taste, along with *lutefisk*, dried and salted ling or cod, steeped in lye. It is traditionally eaten at Christmas time and has a very distinctive taste and aroma – or some would say stench. *Tørrfisk*, or stockfish, is a tremendously popular snack eaten either dry or cooked.

Something else found on many menus along the coast, particularly in the north, might raise a few eyebrows: whale meat. Norwegians, on the whole, don't find it controversial to eat whale, and the history of whaling goes back a long time in the north of the country. Whale steak, whale burgers and the like are found in many restaurants, although less so now since the whale hunting quota has been cut.

Sami Cooking

Traditional Sami cooking, much like Norwegian cooking in general, was based around what was available and what the land could yield at different times of year. However, many Sami were in the past largely self-sufficient and lived on the fish or meat they themselves could catch. Although much has changed in terms of Sami lifestyle over the last century, many of the staples in Sami cooking have remained. Arctic char is still one of the best-loved fish, and reindeer still forms part of the diet. All parts of the animal, from marrow to blood, are used. *Renkok*, or reindeer stew, is still a popular dish, and black pudding is made with reindeer blood and flour. Reindeer also used to be milked, and dairy products such as cheese were produced.

Presentation can be nearly as important as taste

Shellfish, although only commonly eaten since the latter part of the 20th century, has taken off in a big way and Norwegians are now great consumers of seafood, including the Arctic prawn, lobsters, oysters, mussels, scallops and crabs. The enormous red king crab, caught near the North Cape, is particularly good. In summer, crab parties, *krabbelag*, are held where the crabs are eaten just with rustic bread, butter and perhaps a lemon wedge.

But it is not all fish and seafood in Norway – there are also plenty of meat dishes, and dairy products are ever-popular. For the carnivore, Norway has a lot to offer the adventurous. There are reindeer dishes in the north, and elk, including *gravet elg*, a sugar- and salt-cured elk dish, using the same procedure as for *gravlaks*. Pork, beef, chicken, lamb and mutton are also widely used. Meatballs, *kjøttekaker*, are popular, often with a tart lingonberry sauce or relish. Mutton stew with cabbage, *fårikål* (literally 'mutton in cabbage'), is

Fresh berries form the basis of many Norwegian desserts

a warming winter dish, served with potatoes. Sausages of all kinds, including reindeer and elk salamis, or the simple hot dogs, *varme pølser*, are often sold as snacks from kiosks or stalls. In many restaurants dishes still retain a seasonal quality, with good fresh berries in summer and early autumn for the desserts, sauces or marinades, followed by a wide variety of mushroom dishes slightly later in the year, excellent game in autumn and hearty stews, soups and casseroles in winter.

Vegetables do not figure prominently on menus, however, and this can make finding good options a bit tricky for vegetarian visitors, and particularly for vegans, but even this is beginning to change, at least in the bigger cities.

Bread accompanies many meals, and it is usually of the whole grain variety, and a sandwich in Norway tends to be the open kind – just one slice of bread, piled high with all kinds of goodies.

Desserts tend to focus on fresh berries, with cream or ice cream, and waffles are a Norwegian institution, served with clotted cream and a variety of berry jams to choose from – strawberries, cloudberries, raspberries and blueberries being the most popular options.

What to Drink

Norwegians love their coffee: in fact they are the world's leading consumers, downing some 160 litres (35 gallons) per person per year. Having a coffee break, meeting friends and family for coffee and cake, or just having a large mug of coffee at any time of day, could all be considered Norwegian pastimes. There is even an alcoholic kind of coffee, known as *karsk*, which originated in Trøndelag. This usually has a dash of vodka or, more often than not, moonshine spirit, added to it.

Tea has become more common in recent years and there is usually a decent selection of teas available in shops, hotels and restaurants. Soft drinks and fruit juices, either national or international brands, are widely available and popular. Also, in rural areas, many people still prefer to drink a large glass of milk with their meal.

Norway is well known internationally for its strict alcohol policy, but despite this, Norwegians do like to drink. The state-run monopoly, *Vinmonopolet*, is the only kind of shop licensed to sell alcohol for home consumption, and even though prices can be quite expensive, due to the high taxes, they are far more reasonable than the prices for alcoholic drinks bought in bars and restaurants.

Norway has long been a beer-drinking nation and there are various national brews, such as Ringnes from Oslo, Hansa from Bergen, CB from Kristiansand, and Mack, from the world's northernmost brewery, based in Tromsø. Norway also makes distilled spirits of the stronger kind; akvavit (*akevitt*) and vodka. Vikingfjord is Norway's own brand of premium vodka. Akvavits such as Gammel Opland, Linie and Gilde are

Strong tastes

Norwegians like their coffee black – no milk, no sugar, and a very large mug. And it hasn't made them a nation of insomniacs.

Norwegians enjoy convivial evenings out with friends

well-known Norwegian brands, and the tradition of drinking akvavit is mostly associated with Christmas. The rest of the year other, more international, spirits are consumed. Wine is becoming more popular, but it remains comparatively expensive. In fact, drinking wine with your meal in a restaurant can sometimes more than double your bill. It is fairly common, especially in rural areas, to encounter moonshine – *hjemmebrent* – a strong spirit, usually potato-based.

TO HELP YOU ORDER

Restaurant	**restaurant**
A table for..., please	**et bord til..., takk**
I'd like a/an/some...	**Jeg vil gjerne ha en/ett/noen...**
I don't eat meat/	**Jeg spiser ikke kjøtt/**
I'm a vegetarian	** Jeg er vegetarianer**
Could I have the bill, please?	**Kan jeg få regningen, takk?**

beer	**øl**		pepper	**pepper**
bread	**brød**		potatoes	**poteter**
breakfast	**frokost**		red/	**rød/**
butter	**smør**		white wine	**hvitvin**
coffee	**kaffe**		salad	**salat**
cream	**fløte**		salt	**salt**
dessert	**dessert**		sandwich	**smørebrød/**
dinner	**middag**			**sandwich**
fish	**fisk**		soup	**suppe**
lunch	**lunsj**		starter	**forrett**
main course	**hovedrett**		sugar	**sukker**
meat	**kjøtt**		vegetables	**grønnsaker**
milk	**melk**		water	**vann**

MENU READER

blåbær	blueberries		**kjøttkaker**	meatballs
blåskjell	mussels		**krabbe**	crab
bringebær	raspberries		**kylling**	chicken
dyrekjøtt	venison		**lefse**	flatbread
egg	egg			made from
elg	elk/moose			potato
fårikål	mutton stew		**multer**	cloudberries
fiskesuppe	fish soup		**oksekjøtt**	beef
geitost	goat's cheese		**pølser**	sausages
gravlaks	salt and sugar		**rein**	reindeer
	cured salmon		**reker**	shrimp/prawn
hummer	lobster		**sauekjøtt**	mutton
is	ice cream		**skalldyr**	seafood
jordbær	strawberries		**sopp**	mushrooms
kake	cake		**svinekjøtt**	pork
klippfisk	salted and		**sursild**	pickled herring
	dried		**torsk**	cod
	stockfish		**tyttebær**	lingonberries

PLACES TO EAT

We have used the following symbols to give an idea of the price for a three-course meal for one, not including alcohol:

$$$** over NOK700   **$$** NOK300–700   **$ below NOK300

The area of **Aker Brygge**, on the harbour front, has a wide variety of restaurants that are popular year-round, but it is particularly buzzing in summer, when many of the 40-odd establishments have outdoor seating. See www.akerbrygge.no for a full list of restaurants and bars. Another good area for food, particularly at lunch time, is along **Karl Johans Gate**, the main street, running through the centre.

De Fem Stuer $$$ *Kongeveien 26, N-0787 Oslo, tel: 22-92 27 34.* A top-class international restaurant housed within Holmenkollen Park Hotel, a 100-year old building near the Holmenkollen ski centre.

Eataly $–$$ *Bryggetorget 18, N-0250 Oslo, tel: 22-83 13 00, www.eataly.no.* Good-quality Italian restaurant. Large, gorgeous pizzas and pasta dishes; children's portions, and wine by the glass. Lovely outdoor seating, overlooking Aker Brygge and Tjuvholmen, and a central fireplace for winter days. The outdoor seats have sheepskins to sit on and blankets to wrap up in, should it get chilly even on a summer's evening.

Frognerseteren Restaurant and Café $–$$$ *Holmenkollveien 200, N-0791 Oslo, tel: 22-92 40 40, www.frognerseteren.no.* Café Seterstua and Restaurant Finstua are both located in this historic building on the way to Holmenkollen ski jump, overlooking Oslo. Finstua serves first-rate Norwegian cuisine for lunch and dinner; Café Seterstua, which opens at 11am, is more casual. Frognerseteren is very popular with local people, and is reached by tram from central Oslo.

Kaffistova $ *Rosenkrantz gate 8 N-0159 Oslo, tel: 23-21 42 10.*
You will get hearty, wholesome Norwegian home-cooking at reasonable prices at this café-diner in the recently refurbished Hotel Bondeheimen.

Solsiden $$$ *Søndre Akershus kai 34 N-0150 Oslo, tel: 22-33 36 30, www.solsiden.no.* One of the best fish and seafood restaurants in Oslo, this converted warehouse right on the waterfront is open May–September only, but remains ever-popular.

Theatercafeen $$$ *Stortingsgata 24-26 N-0161 Oslo, tel: 22-82 40 50.* This legendary Viennese-style café has been popular with diners for over 100 years. The place to eat and to be seen, good for celebrity-spotting – and the food is excellent too.

THE SOUTH AND SOUTHEASTERN BORDERLANDS

Fredriksten Kro $$ *Fredriksten Fortress (Festning) N-1769 Halden, tel: 69-17 52 32.* Traditional inn near the fortress overlooking Halden. Serves 53 different types of sandwiches and there is a special cake menu.

Sjøhuset Restaurant $$ *Østre Strandgate 12A N-4610 Kristiansand, tel: 38-02 62 60.* Excellent seafood restaurant housed in a former salt storage warehouse. Does a special summer menu and seasonal fare, and there are good fish and chips.

Tollboden Café & Restaurant $$–$$$ *P.A. Heuchsgate 4, N-3770 Kragerø, tel: 35-98 90 90, www.tollboden.org.* Converted 19th-century ship's cabin that serves Italian, French and Nordic-inspired cuisine. Interestingly, also has a special menu for dogs.

STAVANGER AND AROUND

Bølgen & Moi Stavanger $$–$$$ *Norwegian Petroleum Museum, Kjeringholmen, N-4013 Stavanger, tel: 51-93 93 51.* Popular brasserie (with several branches in other parts of Norway), located inside one of Stavanger's most unusual museums.

Food Story $ *Hospitalgata 15, N-4013 Stavanger and Løkkeveien 41 N-4008 Stavanger.* Café and deli with fair-trade and organic products.

Sjøhuset Skagen $$$ *Skagenkaien 16, N-4006 Stavanger, tel: 51-89 51 80, www.sjohusetskagen.no.* Good-quality Norwegian and international food is on the menu in a historic building dating from the 18th century. Part of the *Taste the Coast* network of restaurants.

BERGEN AND AROUND

Altona Vinbar $$ *Strandgaten 81, N-5004 Bergen, tel: 55-30 40 72.* In an historic wine cellar, this is Bergen's oldest tavern, now also serving good food. It's dark, cosy and intimate, perfect for romantic dinners. The seafood is particularly good, as, of course, is the wine list.

Bergen Fish Market $ *Fisketorget, Torget i Bergen, tel: 55-55 20 00 (near the tourist information office), www.torgetibergen. no.* Bergen fish market, teeming with stalls selling all kinds of fish and seafood, is an attraction and an experience in itself. You can pick up excellent lunch-time snacks, fresh from the sea – anything from smoked salmon baguettes to huge seafood trays, to be enjoyed on the spot or as a takeaway. Some of the stalls have wooden benches for seating.

Bryggeloftet & Stuene $$ *Bryggen 11, N-5003 Bergen, tel: 55-30 20 70, www.bryggeloftet.no.* Situated in historic Bryggen, a Unesco World Heritage Site, this place has been run by the same family for generations, and offers Norwegian cooking at its finest. There are traditional '*lutefisk* parties', game dishes, and there are lovely views over the fish market.

Fløien Folkerestaurang $$–$$$ *Fløyfjellet 2, N-5014 Bergen, tel: 55-32 18 75.* Originally opened in 1925, this restaurant at the top of Mount Fløyen, reached by the Fløibanen funicular, has Bergen's most spectacular views and offers innovative Norwegian cooking. Well worth the trip.

Ringheim Café, Tre Kokker Voss $–$$ *Vangsgata 34, N-5703 Voss, tel: 56-51 13 65.* Old-fashioned café with good lunch-time meals at reasonable prices.

CENTRAL NORWAY AND THE WESTERN FJORDS

Gamletorvet Spiseri $$–$$$ *Øvre Torvgate 24, N-2815 Gjøvik, tel: 61-17 04 44.* Housed in the old working men's club, this rustic restaurant serves contemporary and traditional Norwegian dishes and is part of the Historical Hotels and Restaurants of Norway.

Hallingstuene $$$ *Geilovegen 56, opposite the railway station, Geilo, tel: 32-09 12 50, www.hallingstuene.no.* This cosy restaurant, complete with open fires and traditional paintings, is run by a Norwegian celebrity chef and his wife. Specialities include ptarmigan and game dishes, as well as 'Halling tapas' using produce from the area.

Hardanger Saft-og Siderfabrikk, Lekve Gardsrestaurant $–$$ *Lekve Gard, N-5730 Ulvik, tel: 56-52 61 61.* Local gourmet food in lovely setting, in a cider factory. The restaurant is open in summer only; advance booking essential. There is also a café with snacks and cider tastings.

Hummer & Kanari $$–$$$ *Kongensgate 19, N-6002 Ålesund, tel: 70-12 80 08.* Restaurant and bistro serving modern European food with an Italian twist. Good pasta and seafood.

TRØNDELAG AND NORDLAND

Bacalao $–$$ *Kirkegata 23, N-8300 Svolvær, Lofoten Islands, tel: 76-07 94 00.* Nice bistro with soups, sandwiches and salads, in a harbour setting. Terrace seating and a fireplace for when it gets chilly.

Bari $$ *Munke Gata 25, N-7011 Trondheim, tel: 73-60 60 24, www.bari.no.* Trendy, comfy café with changing daytime and evening menus. Italian cooking and Norwegian seafood.

Bella Bulldog $ *Ravelsveita 6, Trondheim, tel: 73-53 38 88, www.bellabulldog.no.* Popular, light and airy lunch-time eatery with hearty home-made soups and sandwiches. They also specialise in the so-called *vækter'n-bolle*, a bread roll with sweet, brown goat's cheese.

Bjørk $$ *Storgata 8, 2nd floor, Bodø, tel: 75-52 40 40, www. restaurantbjork.no.* Café, bar and restaurant with balcony seating in summer, inside Glasmagasinet, Bodø's main mall. Space for pre-dinner drinks or an after-work cocktail. Lunch-time buffet on Friday. Good sushi and pizzas.

Børsen Spiseri $$ *Svinøya Rorbuer, Gunnar Bergs vei 2, N-8300 Svolvær, Lofoten Islands, tel: 76-06 99 30, www.svinoya. no.* Housed in the main reception building of Svinøya's traditional fishing cabin company, Børsen offers traditional Lofoten cuisine, in a rustic romantic setting, overlooking the fjord. The Taste of Lofoten plate serves as a good introduction to the islands' cuisine, including Lofoten lamb, stockfish, whale and even some local cheeses.

Bryggeri Kaia $$ *Sjøgaten 1, Bodø, tel: 75-52 58 08, www. bryggerikaia.no.* Bodø's best eatery, set right on the harbour – grilled-meat buffet, speciality tapas and seafood platters to choose from. Outdoor seating by the waterfront and a piano bar functions at the weekends.

Fairytale Cupcakes $ *Repslagerveita 2B, N-7012 Trondheim, tel: 40-05 61 08, www.fairytalecupcakes.no.* Lovely little café in central Trondheim, taking the fairy-tale theme to new heights. The decor is all in pastels with Baroque-inspired furniture. The cupcakes can be custom-made and come in all flavours from caramel and carrot to tiramisu and raspberry – there is even a 'salty cupcake'.

Havfruen $$ *Kjøpmannsgata 7, N-7013 Trondheim, tel: 73-87 40 70, www.havfruen.no.* Trondheim's premier fish and seafood restaurant, housed in one of the old buildings along Nidelva River. Excellent food in a lovely setting.

Skjærbrygga $$ *N-8340 Stamsund, Lofoten Islands, tel: 76-05 46 00, www.skjaerbrygga.no.* Rustic dining experience at Stamsund's pub-restaurant attached to their fishing cabin accommodation, *rorbuer.* This is the place to try whale steak, *bacalao,* stockfish or the fresh catch of the day. There is an all-day pub menu and an evening à la carte option.

Vertshuset Røros $$–$$$ *Kjerkgata 34, N-7374 Røros, tel: 72-41 93 50, www.vertshusetroros.no.* Situated in a traditional inn, this restaurant emphasises organic food and fresh, local produce. Sample menus include a Taste of Central Norway. The inn serves breakfast, lunch and dinner daily, and also has accommodation (16 double rooms and seven apartments).

THE FAR NORTH

Arctic Restaurant & Bar $$ *Rica Arctic Hotel Kongensgate 1-3, N-9915 Kirkenes, tel: 78-99 59 00, www.rica.no/arctic.* Arctic and international cuisine inside the modern Rica Arctic Hotel in the town centre. À la carte menu; open for breakfast, lunch and dinner.

Emmas Drømmekjøkken $$–$$$ *Kirkegata 8, Tromsø, tel: 77-63 77 30, www.emmas.as.* The name literally means 'Emma's Dream Kitchen'. Innovative cooking, beautifully presented, with new takes on Norwegian classics, run by an excellent team of female chefs.

Kongsfjord Gjestehus $$ *Veines, N-9982 Kongsfjord, tel: 78-98 10 00, www.kongsfjord-gjestehus.no.* Home-cooked, traditional Norwegian dishes with an emphasis on fish and seafood dishes. Marinated whale steak is sometimes on the menu. Local cloudberries and home-made cheesecake are on the dessert menu.

Thai House Restaurant $$ *Storgata 22, N-9008 Tromsø, tel: 77-67 05 26, www.thaihouse.no.* Unusual though it sounds, this is authentic Thai cooking in the Arctic. Open for lunch and dinner. Eat in or takeaway food. Also has a sister restaurant of the same name in Tromsø.

A–Z TRAVEL TIPS

A Summary of Practical Information

A

ACCOMMODATION (see also CAMPING, YOUTH HOSTELS and the list of RECOMMENDED HOTELS starting on page 134)

The standard of hotels is generally good in Norway with a range of comfortable accommodation available. Prices can be quite steep, since many hotels are geared towards the business traveller. There are considerable discounts in summer or at weekends, when hotels do special offers to attract business customers. In recent years smaller, family-run hotels have been bought up by international chains. This does not appear to have worsened the standard, and if anything it has made prices somewhat more competitive. Bear in mind the main tourist season in Norway is quite short and not all accommodation options are available year-round, although this is changing.

As well as hotels there are a number of other accommodation options, in rural areas in particular, such as guesthouses and B&Bs, farm- and home-stays, youth hostels, campsites and, perhaps the most popular of all, a cottage, cabin or holiday home, the so-called *hytte*. Networks such as the Historic Hotels and Restaurants, *De Historiske* (www.dehistoriske.com), have a number of unusual character hotels across the country. In some parts along the coast, for example the Lofoten Islands, it is possible to stay in old fishing cabins, *rorbuer*, or even in a lighthouse. Norway's most extensive hotel pass is the Fjord Pass, offering discounts at 170 places nationwide, www.fjordtours.com. The Norwegian Tourist Board has good advice on places to stay and there is an online booking service at www.visitnorway.com.

I'd like a single/double room.	**Jeg vil gjerne ha et enkelt/dobbeltrom**
with bath/shower	**med bad/dusj**
How much is the room?	**Hvor mye koster rommet?**

AIRPORTS

Norway's main airports are Oslo Gardermoen, Bergen Flesland, Stavanger Sola and Trondheim Værnes. Oslo is also served by Torp near Sandefjord. Because of the distances and topography, domestic flights are a good option for getting around and the country is well served by domestic carriers. There are 16 primary airports, several of which are served by international flights, and 29 regional airports. Taxis from the main airports tend to be quite expensive.

Oslo Gardermoen is 50km (31 miles) north of the city centre and has only one terminal serving both domestic and international flights. There are plenty of eateries, duty-free shops, exchange facilities, tourist information and a car hire desk. The quickest way to the centre of Oslo is the Gardermoen Line Airport Express Train, *Flytoget*, taking 19 minutes and running six times an hour to the Central Station. There are also regular commuter trains operated by Norwegian State Railway, airport coaches and a taxi rank outside the airport (www.oslo.no). Ryanair and other low-cost carriers fly into **Torp** airport, near Sandefjord, 110km (68 miles) south of Oslo. Coaches are laid on to coincide with the flights and take approximately 2–2½ hours. There are also trains to Sandefjord with a bus shuttle to the airport (www.torp.no).

Bergen Flesland is 20km (12 miles) south of Bergen. It has all the usual facilities. A frequent airport bus runs from the bus station and the central Radisson hotels to the airport, taking approximately half an hour (www.bergen-guide.com).

Stavanger Sola lies 15km (9 miles) southwest of the centre and has a conference centre plus the usual facilities. The airport bus takes 20–30 minutes and there are taxis (tel: 67-03 10 00, www.avinor.no).

Trondheim Værnes, 35km (22 miles) north of Trondheim centre, has shops and restaurants, a hotel, meeting and conference facilities, as well as exchange facilities. The airport can be reached by train, airport express bus, regular bus service or taxi. Travel time is around 35–40 minutes (tel: 67-03 25 00, www.avinor.no).

Where can I get a taxi?	Hvor kan jeg finne en taxi?
How much is it to downtown Oslo?	Hvor mye koster det til Oslo sentrum?
Does this bus/train go to Oslo?	Går denne bussen/dette toget til Oslo?

B

BICYCLE HIRE

Bikes are easy to rent, from specialist rental shops or local tourist offices, guesthouses and hotels. Roads tend to be fairly empty and the bigger cities have cycle paths. Bear in mind that the mountain terrain can be challenging. Towns and villages are sometimes few and far between, particularly in the far north, and the weather is very changeable. Rental prices vary widely, depending on the quality of the bike and the area – anything from NOK60–350 a day. Tourist offices usually have good maps and information on bike routes. Two scenic routes are the North Sea Cycle Route and the Navvies' Road. Bike Norway has further information, www.bike-norway.com.

BUDGETING FOR YOUR TRIP

Prices differ between the cities and rural areas, as well as from high season to low season, and prices given here are only approximate. As a rule the cities tend to be more expensive than the countryside, with a few exceptions such as around the best-known fjords.

Car hire. Prices vary considerably. Rates for seven days' hire vary from around NOK2,800 for a small car to NOK3,700 for a large car. Most companies provide child seats, for an additional charge.

Hotels. Average rates per night can be divided into budget, medium and up-market (based on two people sharing and including breakfast): NOK1,100, NOK1,100–1,800 and over NOK1,800. Prices can be well below the NOK1,100 bracket, but also rise well above NOK1,800. There are plenty of special offers, weekend rates and packages for visitors.

Meals and drinks. Breakfast in a café or restaurant costs NOK50–80; lunch NOK60–120; dinner at a medium-priced restaurant, not including drinks, NOK200–250 per head; coffee or soft drink NOK20–30; bottle of wine from NOK150; spirits (4cl) NOK80. Hotel breakfasts and lunches are both good bets, as the former is substantial and restaurants often do a dish of the day at lunch time.

Museums. NOK30–80. Children usually get 50 percent discount.

Petrol. NOK12.20 per litre and diesel NOK11.20. Most petrol stations have automatic pumps that take notes and credit/debit cards.

Public transport. Transport is comparatively expensive in Norway, but both buses and trains are of a high standard of comfort. The average price for a train ticket Oslo–Bergen is NOK600.

Taxis. Taxis are expensive. Average cost from Gardermoen Airport to Oslo city centre is NOK610–720, depending on the time of day.

Tourist cards. The Oslo Pass and the Bergen Card are cards giving free entry to a variety of sights, plus access to free public transport and many other benefits. For further information see www.visit oslo.com and www.visitbergen.com. Visit Norway has information on all passes and tourist cards, www.visitnorway.com.

C

CAMPING

Norway has some 1,000 campsites, graded from one to five stars. Most campsites are open June–August only, with a few open longer, including year-round for caravans and mobile homes. Many sites also have cabins for hire on a weekly basis in summer. Costs for camping range from NOK80–150 per day with an additional fee for electricity hook-up. The Norwegian Camping Card and the Scandinavian Camping Card can be bought at all participating sites and offer discounts, swift registration at sites and other advantages. A Camping Card International is accepted as an equivalent. Both www.camping.no and www.norwaydirect.com have useful information. Norway's Right of Public Access law means you may put up a tent or sleep under stars anywhere in the countryside in open, unfenced land, for a maximum of 48 hours, as long as you are at least 150m/yds from the nearest house or cabin. If you want to stay longer you need the owner's permission. Also bear in mind that open fires are not allowed near forested areas 15 April–15 September.

CAR HIRE

All the major car hire companies are represented in Norway, including Avis, Europcar and Hertz, and there are also local Norwegian car hire firms with competitive rates. Most towns of any size have car hire companies, or cars can easily be hired directly at airports, either booked in advance or upon arrival. Rates are generally cheaper the longer you hire the car for, and there are often special rates in summer or at weekends. It's usually possible to pick up a hire car in one place and drop it off in another. To hire a car you will need a full valid licence from your country of residence, held for at least a year. If a non-EU citizen, you may need an International Driver's Permit (IDP). You must be at least 19 years of age to hire a car, but if you are under 25 years of age you may need to pay a young driver's fee of approximately NOK100 per day. Insurance is mandatory so check that this is included in the cost of the car hire.

I'd like to rent a car.	**Jeg vil gjerne leie en bil.**
tomorrow	**i morgen**
for one day/week	**for en dag/uke**
Please include full insurance.	**Vær så snill og inkludere komplett forsikring.**

CLIMATE

The Gulf Stream gives Norway a milder climate than the latitude might indicate, with temperatures sometimes reaching 25–30°C (77–86°F) in summer. Temperatures vary widely between winter and summer, north and south, coast and interior, sea level and mountain peaks. The weather is very changeable too, and in many parts of the country they joke about having 'all seasons in one day'. Late June to mid-August, the weather tends to be sunny with temperatures in the mid-20s°C (mid-70s°F) and sea temperatures reaching 15–18°C (59–65°F), except in the far north. This is the time to see the midnight sun in the Arctic regions. Spring and autumn are slightly cooler and wetter. Autumn is when you can start to observe the northern lights, *aurora borealis*, best in October, February and March. In winter a lot of Norway, except the coast, is snow-covered and inland temperatures can drop as low as -40°C (-40°F). It may rain any time of year on the coast, and even in summer temperatures can drop to 10°C (50°F), particularly in the evening. Average daytime temperatures in Celsius:

	Oslo	Bergen	Trondheim	Bodø	Tromsø
Jan	-2.3	2.7	-1.6	-1.3	-3.8
Feb	-1.3	3	-0.7	-0.9	-3.1
Mar	2.4	4.9	2.1	-1	-1
Apr	7.3	8	5.1	3.8	1.7
May	14	12.9	10.5	8.5	6.1
June	17.6	15.1	13.2	11.8	11
July	19.9	16.6	15.3	14.1	13.7
Aug	18.7	16.3	14.9	13.8	12.5
Sept	13.7	13.3	11.3	10.7	8.4
Oct	8.1	9.8	6.7	6	3.3
Nov	2.3	5.8	1.8	1.7	-1
Dec	-1.4	3.3	-1.1	-0.5	-3

CLOTHING

It's a good idea to wear several layers and be prepared for differences in temperature. Even on a sunny day it's worth having an umbrella and waterproofs, along with sunglasses and sunhat. Norwegians are generally informal, so shorts and a T-shirt are fine for sightseeing on a warm day. Take extra layers for the evening or if taking a boat trip. Good footwear is essential not only for hiking trails and outdoor activities, but for cobblestones in many cities. During winter, thermals, boots, a coat, scarves, gloves and hats are essential.

CRIME AND SAFETY

Norway is a comparatively safe country, with low crime rates, particularly in terms of violent crime, and it's rare that visitors experience any form of crime. In rural areas crime tends to be burglaries or petty theft. Take the same precautions you would at home, look after your belongings, especially in crowded areas and on public transport, and don't walk alone at night in unlit areas of bigger cities.

D

DRIVING

The roads are usually well maintained and quiet, with the exception of the bigger cities, but even there traffic jams are rare. Winter tyres are obligatory in winter (dates vary depending on location). Some roads in the far north are closed in winter. In spring, when the ground frost thaws, some roads can be challenging to drive along. There are also a number of long tunnels, including Europe's longest at 24.5km (15 miles), in the mountainous areas.

Speed limits. The general speed limit is 80km/h (50mph). In residential areas it is 30km/h (18mph); in built-up areas 50km/h (30mph); on dual carriageways and motorways 90 or 100km/h (55 or 62mph). Caravans and trailers may not exceed 80km/h (50mph) even if the local speed limit is higher.

Documents. A full valid licence from your home country, held for at least a year, is required, or an International Driver's Permit if your licence was issued outside the EU/ECA.

Rules. Drive on the right, pass on the left, and give way to traffic from the right, unless otherwise indicated. Seat belts are obligatory, both in front and back seats. Headlights must be dipped at all times. Drink-driving laws are strict and spot checks are common. The alcohol limit is 0.2 milligrams per litre of blood, so it's best to avoid alcohol altogether or you run the risk of being over the limit, which attracts high fines and the risk of losing your licence.

Accidents and breakdowns. You must carry a red warning triangle and yellow fluorescent vest in case of breakdown or accident. For emergency repairs and technical assistance: Norges Automobil-Forbund NAF, tel: 0810-00 505, Falken, tel: 02222 (freephone), or Viking, tel: 06000 (freephone).

Are we on the right road for...?	**Er dette veien til...?**
My car has broken down.	**Bilen min har fått motorstopp.**
There's been an accident.	**Det har vært en ulykke.**
Driving/driver's licence	**førerkort**
Stop	**stopp**
Crossroads	**veikryss**
Dangerous curve/bend	**farlig kurve**
Parking allowed/No Parking	**parkering tillatt/forbutt**
Drive carefully	**Kjør forsiktig**
Bus stop	**bussholdeplass**
Danger	**Fare**
No entry	**Ingen inngang**
No through road/one-way street	**enveisgate**
Roadworks	**veiarbeid**

E

ELECTRICITY

220 volts AC, standard two-pin, round continental plugs. Visitors should bring their own adaptors.

EMBASSIES, CONSULATES AND HIGH COMMISSIONS

Australia: Strandveien 20, N-1366 Lysaker. Limited consular services. Most services are dealt with by the Australian Embassy in Denmark, tel: (+45) 70-26 36 76, www.denmark.embassy.gov.au.

UK: Thomas Heftyes gate 8, N-0244 Oslo, tel: 23-13 27 00, www. britain.no. Mon–Fri 9am–noon only.

US: Henrik Ibsens gate 48, N-0255 Oslo, tel: 22-44 85 50 (for visa enquiries), www.usa.no.

Ireland: Haakon VIIs gate 1, N-0244 Oslo, tel: 22-01 72 00, email: osloembassy@dfa.ie.

Canada: Wergelandsveien 7, N-0244 Oslo, tel: 22-99 53 00, www. canada.no. 8.30am–12.30pm only.

South Africa: Drammensveien 88 C, N-0271 Oslo, tel: 23-27 32 20, www.saemboslo.no.

Unless otherwise indicated, most embassies and consulates are open Mon–Fri 8.30am–4.30pm.

Where can I find the British/American/ Canadian/Australian/ South African embassy?	**Hvor kan jeg finne den britiske/amerikanske/ kanadensiske/australiensiske/ sørafrikanske ambassaden?**

EMERGENCIES

The police can be reached by dialling 112, ambulance and urgent medical assistance on 113 and the fire brigade on 110. For non-urgent police matters dial 02800.

G

GAY AND LESBIAN TRAVELLERS

Both the legal framework and the general attitude towards lesbian, gay, bisexual and transgendered people are fairly liberal in Norway. Most LGBT travellers do not experience any problems or hassle, but bear in mind that Norway is not a very populous country and there isn't much of an LGBT scene or community outside the main cities, and even there, bars and clubs can be a bit thin on the ground. The liberal attitude doesn't always extend to the smaller, more rural communities, although it's rare that anyone experiences any overt discrimination. LLH, the Norwegian LGBT Association, has more information: Valkyriegaten 15A 5th floor, N-0366 Oslo, tel: 023-10 39 39, www.llh.no. Visit Oslo also has an LGBT section on their website, www.visitoslo.com/en/gay-oslo.

GETTING TO NORWAY

Air. Many international carriers have flights to Norway, either direct or via a hub, including SAS, British Airways, Continental Airlines, Norwegian, KLM, Lufthansa and Thai Airways. Domestic flights are operated by SAS, Norwegian and Wideröe.

Sea. There are ferries between Norway and Denmark, operated by Color Line (www.colorline.com), DFDS Seaways (www.dfdsseaways.co.uk), Fjordline (www.fjordline.com) and Stena Line (www.stenaline.co.uk), as well as Oslo to Kiel in Germany and from Strömstad in Sweden to Sandefjord, both operated by Color Line. In Norway there are numerous ferries and boats along the coast: the best known is Hurtigruten, running from Bergen to Kirkenes in the far north (www.hurtigruten.co.uk or www.hurtigruten.com).

Rail. One option for travelling to, from and around Norway is to get a rail pass, such as an Interrail (for Europeans) or Eurail (for non-Europeans) Global Pass. These must be booked before leaving your country and are offered by the Eurail Group via their online agent www.interrailnet.com, or contact European Rail, tel: 020-7619 1083, www.europeanrail.com (for general European rail tickets).

Coach. Eurolines is the leading operator of scheduled coach services from the UK to Europe, and journey times to Oslo are around 40 hours. See www.eurolines.co.uk for further information.

GUIDES AND TOURS

English is widely spoken in Norway, so it is easy to find English-speaking guides and tours. Many bus or boat tours and museums have multilingual guiding in Norwegian, English, German, French and increasingly in Russian, Mandarin and Japanese. Tourist offices can book tours and guides, and provide multilingual leaflets about the tours available. Some of the most popular tours, such as Norway in a Nutshell, are organised by Nutshell Tours and Fjord Tours (www.norwaynutshell.com and www.fjordtours.com). Visit Norway has a useful list of tourist offices at www.visitnorway.com.

| We need an English-speaking guide. | **Vi trenger en engelsktalende guide.** |

H

HEALTH AND MEDICAL CARE

Norway is a member of the EEA (the European Economic Area), which entitles all visitors from other member countries to the same medical care as Norwegian citizens. EU/EEA nationals should bring a European Health Insurance Card (EHIC) available in the UK through post offices or online at www.ehic.org.uk; it is free and valid for five years. Travel insurance is highly recommended for all visitors. Make sure this covers you for winter or adventure sports, if you plan to engage in these. There are no vaccinations required for Norway and tap water is safe to drink.

There is a 24-hour pharmacy *(apotek)* in Oslo: Jernbanetorvet Pharmacy, Jernbanetorget 4B, N-0154 Oslo, tel: 23-35 81 00.

Where can I find the nearest (all-night) pharmacy?	**Hvor kan jeg finne det nærmeste (24-timers) apotek?**
I need a doctor/ dentist/an ambulance	**Jeg trenger en doktor/ tannlege/ambulanse**
hospital	**hospital/sykehus**
I have an upset stomach	**Jeg har mavepine**
a fever	**feber**
headache	**hodepine**
cold/flu	**førkjølelse/influensa**

HOLIDAYS

New Year's Day	1 January
Maundy Thursday	March/April
Good Friday	March/April
Easter Monday	March/April
Labour Day	1 May
Constitution/National Day	17 May
Ascension Day	May/June
Whit Monday	late May/early June
Christmas Day	25 December
Boxing Day	26 December

L

LANGUAGE

Norwegian has two official written forms, *bokmål* (literally 'book language') and *nynorsk* ('new Norwegian'). Some 86 percent primarily use *bokmål*. Across Norway more than 20,000 people also

Hello	**Hei**
Good Morning	**God Morgen**
Good Day	**Goddag**
Good Evening	**God Kveld**
Goodbye	**Ha det**
Yes	**Ja**
No	**Nei**
How are you?	**Hvordan går det?**
I'm fine	**Det går bra**
Nice to meet you	**Hyggelig å treffe deg**
Thank you	**Takk**
You're welcome	**Ingen årsak**
Excuse me	**Unnskyld**
Sorry	**Beklager**
Please	**Vær så snill**
My name is...	**Jeg heter...**
Do you speak English?	**Snakker du engelsk?**
I don't speak Norwegian	**Jeg snakker ikke norsk**
Cheers!	**Skål!**
January	**januar**
February	**februar**
March	**mars**
April	**april**
May	**mai**
June	**juni**
July	**juli**
August	**august**
September	**september**
October	**oktober**
November	**november**
December	**desember**

Monday	**Mandag**
Tuesday	**Tirsdag**
Wednesday	**Onsdag**
Thursday	**Torsdag**
Friday	**Fredag**
Saturday	**Lørdag**
Sunday	**Søndag**

speak various Sami languages, part of the Finno-Ugric language group and not related to Norwegian. English is widely spoken and taught in schools from a young age.

Learning a few useful phrases of Norwegian, although not essential, is very much appreciated. Pronunciation can be a challenge and Norwegian has an additional three vowels, at the end of the alphabet – æ, ø and å. Å is pronounced like the English 'o' in 'cold', æ like 'ai' in 'hair', ø like 'ea' in 'heard'.

M

MAPS

Most local tourist offices have got good maps of their particular area. Another option is Stanfords in the United Kingdom, tel: +44-20 7836 1321, www.stanfords.co.uk.

MEDIA

Radio and television. There are two main television companies, the state-run NRK with four channels, and TV2, also with four channels. All programmes are shown in original language with subtitles. National radio is also dominated by NRK, which has three radio channels broadcasting over FM and DAB.

Newspapers and magazines. According to Reporters Without Borders, Norway ranks number one in worldwide press freedom. The main dailies are *Aftenposten*, *Dagbladet* and *Dagsavisen*, and there is a large number of local newspapers and magazines. *The Norway Post* (www.norwaypost.no) publishes news from Norway in English.

MONEY

Currency. Norwegian currency is the *krone* (plural *kroner*), made up of 100 *øre*. It is abbreviated kr or NOK (the international abbreviation). Coins come in 50 *øre*, 1, 5, 10 and 20 *kroner*. Banknotes come in 50, 100, 200, 500 and 1,000 *kroner*.

Exchange facilities. You can exchange money at airports and at Oslo's Central Station, as well as many commercial and savings banks, some post offices, branches of Forex and some hotels. Forex is the main bureau de change (usually open Mon–Fri 8am–8pm, Sat 9am–5pm).

Credit and debit cards. Most major credit and debit cards are accepted even in smaller establishments. This makes it easier to avoid carrying large quantities of cash. ATMs are easy to find and easy to use and all towns of any size have at least one, but in remote areas it's best to have some cash with you.

Reporting lost or stolen credit cards:
American Express, tel: 0800-68 100

Can I pay by credit card?	**Kan jeg få betale med kredittkort?**
I want to change some money/ pounds/dollars/euros into Norwegian *kroner*.	**Jeg vil gjerne veksle penger/ pund/dollar/euros til norske kroner.**
Where's the nearest bank/ bureau de change?	**Hvor ligger nærmeste bank/ vekselkontor?**
Is there a cash machine/ ATM near here?	**Finnes det en bankomat i nærheten?**
How much does it cost?	**Hvor mye koster det?**

Diners Club, tel: 021-01 50 00
Mastercard, tel: 0800-30 250
VISA, tel: 0815-00 500

Traveller's cheques. Traveller's cheques are gradually becoming less common, but can still be exchanged at banks, Forex and other bureaux de change. Banks usually give better rates.

O

OPENING TIMES

Shops. Most shops are open Mon–Fri 10am–5pm or 6pm, Sat 9am–2pm. Shops in bigger cities and large malls or department stores stay open later, until 8pm or 9pm, and also open on Sunday. Some shops still close for lunch, particularly in rural areas, and it's common for smaller, privately owned shops to close for summer holidays for two weeks or more in July or August.

Banks. Banks are open Mon–Fri 9am–3.30pm, and Thur until 5pm. In the summer months (mid-May–mid-Aug), banks close at 2.30pm all week, but bureaux de change stay open later.

P

POLICE

Most police stations are open weekdays and have a desk where the public can report crime or other incidents. The emergency number for the police is 112 and this is free when calling from a payphone.

Where's the nearest police station?	**Hvor er den nærmeste politistasjon?**
I've lost my wallet /bag/passport /documents.	**Jeg har mistet lommeboken min/ posen min/passet mitt/ dokumenterne mine.**

POST OFFICES

Norwegian postboxes are red for both national and international mail. Most post offices are open Mon–Fri 8am–5pm and Sat 9am–3pm, closed on Sunday.

Where's the nearest post office?	Hvor er nærmeste postkontor?

PUBLIC TRANSPORT

Norway has good public transport connections to most parts of the country, but in some rural areas and the far north, a car or boat can be a necessity for getting from A to B.

By Air. Due to the long distances, flying is one of the best options for getting around Norway. There are some 50 airports, serving even very small communities. The main carriers for domestic flights are SAS (www.flysas.com), Norwegian (www.norwegian.com) and Widerøe (www.wideroe.no).

By Train. Norwegian State Railways, NSB, covers 3,000km (1,864 miles), as far north as Bodø. Several journeys are particularly scenic such as the Bergen Line, from Oslo to Bergen, the Rauma railway from Dombås to Åndalsnes, and the Flåm Railway from Myrdal to Flåm. For information and tickets see www.nsb.no.

By Bus. A number of bus companies operate in Norway, the largest of which is Nor-Way Bussekspress with 40 routes (www.nor-way.no). Tickets can be bought online or at bus stations. You are allowed to take bikes and skis on board buses for a fee, provided there is space. Many buses are scheduled so that they connect with onward-going ferries or intersecting bus routes.

By Ferry/Boat. A myriad ferry and boat companies operate along the coastline. Many of these are express boats or car ferries connecting the fjordlands and the many islands with the mainland. It's often necessary to hop on a ferry across a fjord since this is quicker than driving to the nearest bridge, and many roads have ferry connections. Hurtigruten, Fjord1, Tide, Fjordline, Kolumbus, Rødne Fjordcruise and The Senja Ferries are some of the main operators. **By Car.** *See Driving, page 119.*

Where can I get a taxi?	**Hvor kan jeg finne en taxi?**
Where is the nearest bus stop?	**Hvor er nærmeste bussh oldeplass?**
When's the next bus to...?	**Når går neste buss til...?**
I would like a ticket to...	**Jeg vil gjerne ha en billet til...**
single/return	**enkel/tur-retur**

R

RELIGION

Around 80 percent of the population are Protestants, belonging to the state Lutheran Church. This figure is somewhat misleading as one becomes a member when baptised and in reality Norway is one of the most secular nations in Europe with people attending church only once or twice a year. Some 10 percent of the population do not belong to any organised form of religion and the remainder belong to a variety of faiths from the Sami shamanistic religion to Bahá'i.

T

TELEPHONE

Public phones taking coins, phonecards or credit cards, and are easy to find in main cities and towns. Phonecards are sold in newsagents, 7Elevens and similar stores. Off the beaten track, including the far north, payphones are harder to find. Taking your own mobile, or, for longer stays, buying a Norwegian SIM card, are good options, but beware of steep roaming rates and lack of reception.

TIME ZONE

Norway keeps Central European Time, one hour ahead of Greenwich Mean Time, with Daylight Saving Time from late March to late October, when clocks go forward by one hour.

New York	London	Paris	**Oslo**	Sydney	Auckland
6am	11am	noon	**noon**	8pm	10pm

TIPPING

It is usual to round up a restaurant or bar bill to the nearest 5 or 10 *kroner*, but it's rarely frowned upon if you don't. Ten percent in bars and restaurants is reasonable if you have received good service. Taxi drivers sometimes receive slightly higher tips, whereas tipping is not expected at the hairdressers, for example.

TOILETS

There are plenty of clean, well-kept public toilets in cities; most are coin operated and charge around NOK5. In rural areas toilets are harder to find, but service stations, areas near main squares or tourist offices are usually a good bet and mostly free. Along highways there are lay-bys or rest areas with toilet facilities, but off the beaten track and along smaller roads, toilets are nonexistent.

Excuse me, where is the toilet? **Unnskyld, hvor er toalettet?**

TOURIST INFORMATION

Innovation Norway, the Norwegian Tourist Board, has 17 main tourist information offices in Norway and there is a large number of local tourist information offices across the country, although some are only open in summer. All display the international tourist sign (white 'i' on green background). Staff are knowledgeable, often multilingual, and can provide information about the area and make bookings for accommodation and tours. There are usually also leaflets and maps available in various languages.

In Norway:

Central Station Tourist Information, Trafikanten Service Centre, Jernbanetorget 1, N-0154 Oslo (Mon–Fri 9am–4pm), tel: 81-53 05 55, www.visitoslo.com.

The Norway Information Centre, Fridtjof Nansens Plass 5, N-0160 Oslo, tel: 24-14 77 00, www.visitnorway.com, has information on Oslo and the rest of Norway.

Bergen, Vågsallmenningen 1, N-5003 Bergen, tel: 55-55 20 00, www.visitbergen.com.

Stavanger, Domkirkeplassen 3, N-4006 Stavanger, tel: 51-85 92 00, www.regionstavanger.com.

Tromsø, Kirkegata 2, N-9008 Tromsø, tel: 77-61 00 00, www.visit troms.no.

Trondheim, Munkegata 19, N-7013 Trondheim, tel: 73-80 76 62, www.trondheim.com or www.visit-trondheim.com.

For information on the **Western Fjords**, www.fjordnorway.com.

Overseas:

Innovation Norway has offices in 25 countries worldwide.

In the UK: Innovation Norway, Charles House, 5 Lower Regent Street, London SW1Y 4LR, tel: 020-7839 6255 or 0906-302 2003 (24-hour brochure hotline), www.visitnorway.com.

In the US: Innovation Norway, 655 Third Avenue, New York, NY 10017, tel: 212-885 9700, www.visitnorway.com.

V

VISAS AND PASSPORTS

EU citizens only need a valid passport to visit Norway, which is a member of the Schengen agreement. Visitors from Canada, Australia, USA and New Zealand do not need a tourist visa for stays of under 90 days. Other nationalities should check with their Norwegian embassy. A visitor's visa is usually valid for three months.

WEBSITES AND INTERNET CAFÉS

Most tourist information websites have information in English (and additional languages). The following is a list of useful websites:

www.visitnorway.com

www.visitoslo.com

www.visitbergen.com

www.fjordnorway.no

www.regionstavanger.com

www.trondheim.com or **www.visit-trondheim.com**

www.trondelag.com

www.visitnorthnorway.com

www.lofoten.info

www.bike-norway.com

www.norwegian.com

www.flaamsbana.no

www.hurtigruten.co.uk and **www.hurtigruten.com**

There is internet access at most airports and stations. Hotels, restaurants, cafés and bars increasingly have Wi-fi.

YOUTH HOSTELS

Norway has more than 100 hostels, run by two different chains – Hostelling International (www.hihostels.no) and VIP Backpackers Resorts International (www.backpackers.no). Dormitories range from NOK100–300, a double room from NOK300–600. Hostels usually provide duvets and pillows, but bring your own linen or sleeping bag. Most hostels provide very good value for money.

Recommended Hotels

Norway has a variety of accommodation from luxury establishments to youth hostels, and typically standards are high, often with prices to match. International chains have taken over a number of hotels, but as a rule the character has remained unchanged. Choice hotels (www. choicehotels.no) and Best Western (www.bestwestern.no) tend to be of better quality in Norway than in many other places and have some of the best city locations. In the fjordlands and the countryside there are still many smaller guesthouses and B&B accommodation. Sometimes family-run, they are often more reasonably priced and in scenic settings. Some of the best hotels are members of the Historic Hotels and Restaurants network – manor houses, boutique hotels and old coaching inns, for example (www.dehistoriske.com). Renting a cottage (*hytte*) is also an option, and can reduce accommodation and food costs substantially (www.norsc.co.uk). For those on an even stricter budget, hiring a camper van/mobile home or simply taking a tent is another option. Campsites are plentiful, although the season is short, especially in the far north. In the bigger cities hotels are open year-round, but some smaller guesthouses open only during the summer season.

The price categories are based on two people sharing a double room at full rates including breakfast, MOMS (VAT) and service charge.

$$$	over NOK1,800
$$	NOK1,100–1,800
$	below NOK 1,100

OSLO

Best Western Karl Johan $$ *Karl Johansgate 33, N-0162 Oslo, tel: 23-16 17 00, www.bestwestern.com.* One of the most centrally located hotels in Oslo, opposite parliament, with excellent views.

Clarion Collection Hotel Folketeateret $$ *Storgaten 21–3, N-0184 Oslo, tel: 22-00 57 00, www.choicehotels.no.* Recently opened central hotel with 160 rooms. A light evening buffet is included in the room price.

Cochs Pensjonat $ *Parkveien 25, N-0350 Oslo, tel: 23-33 24 00, www.cochspensjonat.no*. Good-value family-run guesthouse close to the Royal Palace. Three different types of rooms, some with a kitchenette and fridge for self-catering.

First Hotel Grims Grenka $$$ *Kongens Gate 5, N-0153 Oslo, tel: 23-10 72 00, www.firsthotels.com*. Oslo's first design hotel has 50 rooms including six suites, a rooftop lounge for cocktails and a restaurant that serves Scandinavian specialities.

First Hotel Millennium $$$ *Tollbugata 25, N-0157 Oslo, tel: 21-02 28 00, www.firsthotels.com*. Well-appointed hotel a short walk from Karl Johan. There are 112 rooms and excellent conference and meeting facilities.

Hotell Bondeheimen $$$ *Rosenkrantz Gate 8, N-0159 Oslo, tel: 23-21 41 00, www.bondeheimen.com*. The 127 rooms in this central hotel have been recently renovated. The 100-year-old café, Kaffistova, serves traditional Norwegian cuisine and there is a good handicraft shop attached.

THE SOUTH AND SOUTHEASTERN BORDERLANDS

Gaustablikk Hotell $–$$ *N-3660 Rjukan, tel: 35-09 14 22, www.gaustablikk.no*. Mountain lodge at the foot of southern Norway's highest peak. It is a ski centre in winter. Also has cabins sleeping up to 16 people.

Grand Hotell Halden $–$$ *Jernbanetorget 1, N-1767 Halden, tel: 69-18 72 00, www.grandhotell.net*. The oldest hotel in Halden, dating from the 1850s, the Grand has 33 rooms. At the time of writing these were being extensively refurbished and upgraded.

Rica Hotel Norge $$ *Dronningens Gate 5, N-4666 Kristiansand, tel: 38-17 40 00, www.hotel-norge.no*. Centrally located hotel with good spa facilities. Also does cooking courses in the Gladkjøkkenet restaurant.

Clarion Collection Hotel Amanda $$ *Smedasundet 93, N-5501 Haugesund, tel: 52-80 82 00, www.choicehotels.no.* Intimate hotel offering organic breakfasts and a light evening buffet. Sauna and health club facilities.

Energihotellet $–$$ *N-4244 Nesflaten, tel: 51-20 05 55, www.energihotellet.no.* Recently spruced-up design hotel with 14 double rooms, overlooking Suldalsvatnet Lake.

Rogalandsheimen Gjestgiveri $ *Muségate 18, N-4010 Stavanger, tel: 51-52 01 88, www.rogalandsheimen.no.* Open since 1890, with 15 individually designed rooms. TV room on the second floor.

Skagen Brygge Hotell $$$ *Skagenkaien 28–30, N-4004 Stavanger, tel: 51-85 00 00, www.skagenbryggehotell.no.* In the heart of the harbour, one of the best locations in Stavanger. Good atmosphere and excellent cocktail bar facing the quayside.

Stavanger Bed & Breakfast $ *Vikedalsgaten 1A, N-4012 Stavanger, tel: 51-56 25 00, www.stavangerbedandbreakfast.no.* Budget accommodation a short walk from the cathedral; 22 rooms. Free Wi-fi, bumper breakfasts and coffee with waffles in the evenings.

Augustin Hotel $–$$ *C. Sundts Gate 22, N-5004 Bergen, tel: 55-30 40 00, www.augustin.no.* Centrally located with 113 rooms; free Wi-fi and free waffles. Cosy basement wine bar and restaurant.

Grand Hotel Terminus $$ *Zander Kaaesgate 6, N-5015 Bergen, tel: 55-21 25 00, www.ght.no.* Elegant hotel near the station. It has reputedly the best whisky bar in Norway; there are stone-baked pizzas as well as gourmet dining.

Hanseatic Hotel Bergen (Det Hanseatiske Hotel) $–$$ *Finnegården 2A, Rosenkrantzgaten 6, N-5809 Bergen, tel: 55-30 48*

00, www.dethanseatiskehotell.no. Within the Bryggen Unesco World Heritage Site; 16 individual rooms with classic wooden interiors.

Sandven Hotel $$ *N-5602 Norheimsund, tel: 56-55 20 88, www. sandvenhotel.no*. Worth a visit for its 150-year history alone. Beautifully restored to its former glory by owner Tron Bach, it has 33 individually designed rooms and a floating café on Hardangerfjord.

Solstrand Fjord Hotel $$$ *Osøyro, N-5200 Os, tel: 56-57 11 00, www.solstrand.com*. Beautiful historic hotel and spa on the Bjørnefjord, 30km (19 miles) south of Bergen. Outdoor and indoor pools and a variety of treatments available.

CENTRAL NORWAY AND THE WESTERN FJORDS

Brakanes Hotel $$ *N-5730 Ulvik, Hardanger, tel: 56-52 61 05, www.brakanes-hotel.no*. A grand old dame of a hotel with 143 comfortable rooms, many with balconies overlooking the fjord.

Dr Holms Hotel $$$ *Timrehaugveien 2, N-3580 Geilo, tel: 32-09 57 00, www.drholms.no*. Member of the Historic Hotels network, it has a long and distinguished history. The 127 rooms are all decorated in English romantic style and the spa is renowned.

Fossheim Turisthotell $–$$ *N-2688 Lom, tel: 61-21 95 00, www. fossheimhotel.no*. Traditional hotel in an old-fashioned wooden building. Gourmet dining; good walking in nearby Jotunheimen national park. Closed mid-December to mid-February.

Hotel Brosundet $$ *Apotekergata 5, N-6004 Ålesund, tel: 70-11 45 00, www.brosundet.no*. Room options include the Molja lighthouse on the harbour. The restaurant serves excellent seafood.

Quality Hotel $$ *Gravensteinsgata 5, N-6851 Sogndal, tel: 57-62 77 00, www.choicehotels.no*. Large, well-equipped hotel a short walk from Sogndal bus station. Three restaurants with a wide choice of dishes, from pizzas to Norwegian specialities.

Tørvis Fjord Hotel $$ *N-6873 Marifjøra, tel: 57-68 72 00, www. torvis.no*. Old-fashioned, white-painted building in a manor-house style, complete with well-kept gardens for alfresco meals. Situated right on the Lustrafjord near a small beach and pier.

Vangsgaarden Guesthouse $ *N-5745 Aurland, tel: 57-63 35 80, www.vangsgaarden.no*. A cluster of quaint buildings in the village of Aurland, it includes a guesthouse, a motel, pub and several fjord cabins *(rorbuer)*, beautifully situated on the Aurlandsfjord.

Walaker Hotel $$ *N-6879 Solvorn, tel: 57-68 20 80, www.walaker. com*. Norway's oldest family-run hotel has been in the hands of the same family since 1690. It is part of the Historic Hotels network and has rooms in the main building, in the annex and in a small cottage nearby. Well known for its romantic garden and home-cooked local specialities.

TRØNDELAG AND NORDLAND

Å Rorbuer & Brygga Restaurant $–$$ *Å i Lofoten, N-8392 Sørvågen, Lofoten Islands, tel: 76-09 11 21, www.lofoten-info.no/ aarorbu.htm*. These picturesque fishing cabins, painted a bright red, are situated in one of Lofoten's most authentic old fishing villages, with 33 listed buildings and several of the islands' best museums.

Britannia Hotel $$ *Dronningens Gate 5, N-7011 Trondheim, tel: 73-80 08 00, www.britannia.no*. The oldest hotel in Trondheim, built in 1897, gets its name from the era when British aristocracy came here for a spot of salmon fishing. It retains its classically elegant style in the 247 rooms, including 11 suites, but internet access, cable TV and a fitness and spa centre have been added.

Clarion Collection Hotel Grand Olav $$ *Kjøpmannsgate 48, N-70 10 Trondheim, tel: 73-80 80 80, www.choicehotels.no*. This centrally located hotel, a short walk from the main square and the Nidelva River, is known as Backstage Hotel since most rooms are individually decorated by different artists. Free Wi-fi, DVDs in the rooms, and organic breakfasts.

Quality Hotel Grand Royal $$ *Kongensgate 64, N-8514 Narvik, tel: 76-97 70 00, www.choicehotels.no.* This central Narvik hotel has 107 high-quality rooms and two restaurants and can organise killer-whale safaris and fishing trips. In winter it is only a short distance from good skiing, including off-piste.

Rica Nidelven Hotel $$ *Havnegata 1, N-7010 Trondheim, tel: 73-56 80 00, www.rica-hotels.com.* Large, modern hotel, on River Nidelva, near Trondheim's newest shopping area; 348 well-equipped rooms, and the hotel officially has Norway's best breakfast buffet.

Røros Hotell $$ *An-Magrittsvei, N-7374 Røros, tel: 72-40 80 00, www.roroshotell.no.* The largest hotel in the region with 167 rooms. Close to the centre and good hiking trails. Facilities include a dance restaurant, playroom for children, pool and sauna.

Singsaker Sommerhotell $ *Rogerts Gate 1, N-7052 Trondheim, tel: 73-89 31 00, www.sommerhotell.singsaker.no.* Open only in summer (mid-June to mid-Aug), student accommodation during the rest of the year, Singsaker has 104 rooms sleeping 1–4 people, or dormitory style. Breakfast is included.

Skagen Hotel $$ *Nyholmsgata 11, N-8005 Bodø, tel: 75-51 91 00, www.skagen-hotel.no.* Comfortable hotel located in two adjacent buildings, connected by an underground tunnel. Close to the centre; free Wi-Fi.

Skjærbrygga Rorbuer $ *N-8340 Stamsund, Lofoten Islands, tel: 76-05 46 00, www.skjaerbrygga.no.* A collection of 19 former fishing cabins *(rorbuer)*, some more than 100 years old, each sleeping 4–8 people. Beautiful location on Vestfjorden, and it has a lovely restaurant and pub also by the fjord.

Svinøya Rorbuer $–$$ *Gunnar Bergs vei 2, N-8300 Svolvær, Lofoten Islands, tel: 76-06 99 30, www.svinoya.no.* Svinøya has 30 different fishing cabins, from standard to de luxe, situated on a small island near the centre of Svolvær. There is also an excellent restaurant attached to the main building.

THE FAR NORTH

Arctic Cabin $ *Hamna, Syltefjord, N-9990 Båtsfjord, tel: 91-64 24 41, www.arctic-cabin.com.* Scenic cabins and accommodation in a tranquil setting on the Syltefjord. One cabin has an outdoor jacuzzi and there are ample barbecue facilities for summer evenings. A stay can be combined with fishing and birdwatching tours, or king crab safaris *(see What to Do, page 84).*

Kongsfjord Gjestehus $ *Veines, N-9982 Kongsfjord, tel: 78-98 10 00, www.kongsfjord-gjestehus.no.* A converted farmhouse and fishermen's quarters dating back to the end of the 18th century, this guesthouse has a quiet, cosy atmosphere and is open year-round. There is a nearby gallery, and boat trips and diving excursions can also be arranged.

Rica Ishavshotel $$ *Fr Langesgate 2, N-9008 Tromsø, tel: 77-66 64 00, www.rica-hotels.com.* Set right on the harbour, Rica Ishavshotel offers great views of the fjord and the Arctic Cathedral opposite. It has 180 modern, well-appointed rooms, scrumptious breakfasts, and lies within easy walking distance of the main sights.

Stauran Art Café and Accommodation $ *Syltefjord, N-9990 Båtsfjord, tel: 78-98 59 50 or 41-47 88 27, www.syltefjord.no.* Beautiful wooden cabins and camping grounds set in a quiet, unspoilt part of northern Finnmark. Perfect for getting away from it all, with hiking trails on the doorstep. There are good self-catering facilities, and the remarkable stone art café, filled to the brim with unusual stone paintings, also does fantastic waffles.

SVALBARD

Radisson Blu Polar Hotel Spitsbergen $$$ *Road 500, N-9171 Longyearbyen, Svalbard, tel: 79-02 34 50, www.radissonblu.com.* The world's northernmost full-service hotel with 95 rooms and apartment suites. There are unparalleled glacier views, and the hotel can help book and organise Svalbard packages, including outdoor activities and air transport.

INDEX